The

FIELD TRIP

Handbook

A Guide to Visiting Museums

The
FIELD TRIP
Handbook
A Guide to Visiting Museums

Genean Stec
Chester County Intermediate Unit

GoodYearBooks
An Imprint of ScottForesman
A Division of HarperCollins*Publishers*

GoodYearBooks

are available for most basic curriculum subjects plus many enrichment areas. For more GoodYearBooks, contact your local bookseller or educational dealer. For a complete catalog with information about other GoodYearBooks, please write:

GoodYearBooks
ScottForesman
1900 East Lake Avenue
Glenview, IL 60025

Preface

The annual field trip is commonly perceived as the yearly outing dreaded by teachers and celebrated by students. It is a day out of the classroom during which students run wild, dashing through monstrous buildings filled with "old" treasures. Teachers spend the day feeling hassled and disorganized, counting heads, money, and sandwiches, and looking for lost students, jackets, and lunches. At the end of the exhausting day they wonder why they came at all. What was the educational value of this field trip?

This book brings the field trip experience into focus for the classroom teacher, making it a manageable and enjoyable experience for all. It is designed for teachers of kindergarten through eighth grade. This book provides classroom teachers with an assortment of checklists, planning charts, and student activities to help them prepare and carry out well-researched and organized curriculum-based field trips. Step-by-step procedures help to ensure that all the details involved in organizing and conducting a field trip are covered.

The first three sections of the book deal with planning and organizing the field trip experience. The next section details pre-visit, museum, and post-visit student activities. These range in difficulty from very simple perceptual activities to more complex activities that require a higher level of thinking skills, and most of the activities can be easily adapted to meet the special needs and skills of your students. These classroom and museum activities will encourage students to describe, compare, contrast, analyze, probe, discuss, argue, and think. They will also facilitate the development of language skills as students express their ideas and opinions concerning the objects and experiences they encounter in the museum.

The pre-visit activities are designed to be used with the students in the classroom before the field trip. They are designed to introduce the museum topic to the students and to prepare them for their museum visit.

The museum activities are designed to be done at the museum using the museum's collection. They were created to encourage object-based teaching and to help sharpen the students' cognitive and perceptual skills.

The post-visit activities are designed to be done in the classroom after the students return from their field trip. They provide a form of closure to the field trip and will help place the experience into the context of the classroom curriculum.

The final section of the book provides an opportunity for teachers, chaperons, and students to evaluate the educational value of the field trip experience.

An annotated bibliography provides teachers with a wealth of resources, which they can draw upon to enrich the classroom curriculum further.

Acknowledgement

This book was created and produced by Project MEET (Museum Education Enrichment for Teachers), a program sponsored by the Chester County Intermediate Unit. Genean Stec, the MEET Coordinator, and the staff of the Chester County Intermediate Unit contributed their knowledge, skills, and expertise to the development of this book. Project MEET is funded primarily by a generous grant from the William Penn Foundation to improve school participation in museum education.

After working many years for cultural organizations, one comes to know that there is nothing "new" in this world. Many of the concepts and activities included in this resource book reflect the efforts and creative activities of teachers and museum educators from around the United States. The bibliography reflects the work of many of these educators.

Contents

From *The Field Trip Handbook* by Genean Stec, published by Good Year Books. Copyright © 1992 Chester County Intermediate Unit.

From *The Field Trip Handbook* by Genean Stec, published by Good Year Books. Copyright © 1992 Chester County Intermediate Unit.

From *The Field Trip Handbook* by Genean Stec, published by Good Year Books. Copyright © 1992 Chester County Intermediate Unit.

Chapter 1
Museums and Schools Working Together

Today there are more than six thousand museums in the United States engaging in an extraordinary variety of activities. Education is an important function in all museums. Museums offer the visitor alluring ways to learn about the world and the cultures that contribute to it. Nowhere else is such a learning experience available. In schools, the *word* is the principal tool of education. In museums, it is the *object* that enlightens. Words are often too abstract to convey particular experiences. Museums can offer students tangible examples of ideas, processes, histories, and environments and provide visitors with multi-sensory experiences.

Many of a student's most valuable learning experiences take place outside the classroom. Some students learn better by doing, seeing, touching, and manipulating. Museum experiences can provide a powerful adjunct to formal classroom learning. Rather than replacing classroom learning, museums are interested in awakening students' interests, stretching their minds, engaging their senses, and stimulating them to go back to school to learn. By working together, museums and schools can create an outstanding educational experience for students. Teaching directly from original objects can enrich classroom learning and bring it to life. It is important that teachers become aware of the educational opportunities museums have to offer and work to create learning situations that incorporate them into the classroom curriculum.

What Is a Museum?

A *museum* is an institution that collects, preserves, exhibits, and interprets the natural and cultural objects of our world. But such a definition does not capture the wonder or the spirit of a museum visit. Museums are much more than institutions that house collections of objects. They are vibrant places where people can go to learn, to compare themselves to others, to stretch their imaginations, to peer into the past, and to dream about the future.

Interpretation is a critical function of a museum. Without it, the objects and collections of museums would lose their value and meaning.

To use their objects to communicate ideas, museums rely on words (labels) and interpreters. Museums have assumed the tremendous responsibility of interpreting their collections and sharing this knowledge with new generations. In this role, museums have become centers of learning in their own right.

Museums come in all sizes and shapes and are filled with all kinds of collections. Most museums can be organized in three general categories—art, history, and science. Under these categories there are many specialized museums devoted to such subjects as plants, dolls, furniture, glass, rollerskating, stamps, textiles, the environment, industry, technology, and zoology.

The *art museums* of the world over time have acquired vast collections of arts which provide the visitor with aesthetic and emotional pleasure as well as a social document of the times. Art is a way of looking at the world. It reflects the trends, attitudes, morals, and innovations of its time. Art is a tangible form of inspiration, a record of the creative mind.

History museums collect and preserve the past and present. They provide us a means of relating to the past. The objects of history bring to life the attitudes, the social milieus, the technologies, and the people of other eras.

Natural history museums are collectors of the plant and animal life of the past and present. Their collections are often the records of great explorations of continents, oceans, and outer space.

Now that you are familiar with the types of museums, you can begin thinking about what kind of field trip experience you want for your students. The following section discusses the field trip experience. It provides a summary of the types of museum experiences along with planning charts and checklists to help you organize and schedule an enjoyable and meaningful field trip for both you and your students.

From *The Field Trip Handbook* by Genean Stec, published by Good Year Books. Copyright © 1992 Chester County Intermediate Unit.

The Field Trip Experience

Teachers today are faced with increasing demands to meet specific curriculum guidelines in an already overcrowded teaching schedule. Classroom teaching time is seen as a precious commodity to be guarded carefully. Unfortunately, the field trip is often perceived as an annual hassle which disrupts a crowded teaching schedule and reduces precious classroom time. To many teachers, a field trip is an outing taken at the end of a busy school year to release students' pent-up energy. The field trip is a day of fun for students and a day of headaches for teachers.

Museums and schools should be partners in education. The museum experience can enhance and enrich classroom learning. Educators should make every effort to incorporate the multi-sensory experiences that museums offer into classroom learning. In museums, students encounter firsthand the objects of our human-made and natural world. Museum visits help broaden the base of a student's life experience. Much of what students become as adults is greatly influenced by the kinds of learning opportunities they have been exposed to as children. Museum experiences will help students heighten their perceptual skills, cultivate the ability to discriminate, and enrich their knowledge of their own—and others'—cultural heritage.

Field trips to museums can add a valuable educational component to any school curriculum. But it must be stressed that simply going to a museum with your students, whether you participate in a program or self-guide your visit, will not guarantee a beneficial educational experience. *The success of a field trip is based on careful research, thoughtful planning, and an open discussion with the museum educators at the site.* The task of planning and scheduling a field trip should not be delegated to the school secretary or the classroom parent. This is a task that should be handled by the teacher, the one person who clearly knows the needs, limits, skills, and knowledge of his or her students. The information and experiences presented to the students must be relevant to them, otherwise the information is sure to be forgotten.

Many types of museum experiences are available for students. In the last decade, there has been an explosion of educational resources offered by museums to schools. Begin collecting information on your local museums by contacting their museum education departments and initiating dialogues between them and your school. Discover which of the following resources are available to you and your students at your local museums.

Following are descriptions of various types of museum education programs that are available to teachers and students in many museums throughout the country. Call or write to your local museums and inquire as to whether they offer these services or others. Many of these educational services are offered to teachers and students free of charge or for a nominal fee.

Teacher Workshops and In-Service Courses

Many museums sponsor teacher workshops year round. The workshops are often held after school or on weekends. Some museums offer teacher workshops in conjunction with local school districts. These collaborative efforts appeal to teachers because they are often able to receive continuing education credits for participation in these classes. Some museums have sufficient staff to offer teacher workshops and in-service courses at the schools as well as in the museum. Teacher workshops can vary tremendously as to topic and approach. They can:

- introduce teachers to the museum, its facilities, and its educational resources

- provide a "look behind-the-scenes"

- examine new traveling exhibitions

- focus on specific topics or themes

- teach teachers how to incorporate museum resources into the classroom curriculum

Through workshops teachers learn about the vast array of resources museums have to offer. Besides regular schedules of exhibitions and related programs, such resources can include free buses to transport students to and from the museum, loan materials, slide kits, films, videos, written materials, artifacts, student and teacher scholarships, internship programs, and special-needs programs.

Teacher Resource Centers and Libraries

A museum's teacher resource center provides teachers with ways to make the museum's collection more accessible to the students and teachers. These centers are stocked with an abundance of resources such as printed information, posters, reproductions, audiovisual materials, films, videos, slides, filmstrips, cassettes, records, books, models, and suggested lesson plans. The centers are usually open on weekends and on selected weekday evenings. Teachers are generally admitted free of charge to the centers.

Loan Programs

As a result of diminishing field trip budgets and the increasing difficulty of taking students on field trips, many museums have developed loan programs to extend museum resources into the classroom. The programs are typically designed around

From *The Field Trip Handbook* by Genean Stec, published by Good Year Books. Copyright © 1992 Chester County Intermediate Unit.

a particular theme or topic and are organized in trunks or as kits which are either picked up by the teacher at the museum or delivered to the classroom. Loan programs provide students with museumlike experiences in a classroom setting. The trunks or kits typically contain a teacher's guide, artifacts and/or reproductions, models, and audiovisuals. The teacher's guide usually includes lesson plans, student activities, and suggestions of ways to relate the material to the classroom curriculum. All types of museums—art, history, and science—have loan programs. Art and history museums loan out materials such as slide sets, films, photographs, tapes, and quality reproductions. Science museums loan out similar materials with the addition of scientific equipment such as microscopes. Natural history museums loan out study collections including rocks, plants, insects, and stuffed animals. Some zoos loan out animals. Loan programs give students the opportunity to interact with authentic or reproduction objects and even live animals.

Many museum loan programs are tied to particular museum experiences for students such as workshops or special tours. The loan program and its materials provide pre-visit activities to prepare the students for their museum experience.

Outreach to the Schools Programs

Some museums will send trained interpreters or staff members to schools to present classroom and/or auditorium programs to prepare students for upcoming museum field trips and/or to involve them in museumlike experiences if they are not able to visit. These outreach programs often involve hands-on activities for the students along with an audiovisual presentation. Sometimes the museum presenter will bring a loan program, such as a thematic trunk or a mini-exhibition, which can remain on exhibit or in use at the school for a period of time after the presentation.

Mobile Programs and Full-Scale Exhibitions

Mini-van and trailer programs along with full-scale traveling exhibitions designed for school use bring the resources of museums into communities that do not have ready access to museums. These mobile units offer a rich variety of programs both to schools and to the surrounding communities. The programs offered by these mobile units range from live theater to audiovisual presentations, demonstrations, and mini-exhibits. Most include some hands-on participatory activities to involve the audience.

Guided Tours

Guided tours led by trained museum interpreters are still the most popular organized programs that museums offer to schools. The value of guided tours should not be underestimated. Many museum guides or interpreters are trained professional educators, and they can help students develop a visual sensitivity and sharpen their observation skills through the use of proven interpretive techniques and strategies. The museum interpreter is able to supplement and extend the information provided for the visitor on labels and signs in the museum. They are the museum's ambassadors; they can help students and teachers become comfortable in the often overwhelming museum environment.

Under the title "guided tour" fall many different types of tours including:

- single-visit tour programs, which usually last about an hour to an hour and a half, are designed around a particular theme, subject, or curriculum area and are geared to a particular age or grade level. Such visits can only introduce students to the museum and its resources. Single-visit experiences often encourage students to return to the museum later with family and friends for a more in-depth experience.

- multi-visit tour programs, which involve several visits to the museum by students and teachers. Each visit builds upon concepts learned during the previous visit. Multi-visit tour programs provide opportunities for students to focus their studies on particular areas of the collection and to study the collection in greater depth. These tours are usually based on a particular theme, subject, or curriculum area and are geared to a particular age or grade level. This type of tour program is more difficult to participate in because of transportation costs and scheduling problems at school, particularly at the high-school level. Financial support for multi-visit tour programs can often be secured through grants from local businesses.

- tandem tours, which use the resources of several museums based on a particular theme. Students may visit one museum in the morning for a guided program and another in the afternoon for a related guided program. These programs give students a wonderful opportunity to study a topic from two or more perspectives such as history and science or art and science. These are rather rigorous programs are best suited for upper elementary and high-school students.

From *The Field Trip Handbook* by Genean Stec, published by Good Year Books. Copyright © 1992 Chester County Intermediate Unit.

Self-Guided Tours

On a self-guided tour, teachers and their chaperons lead the students through the museum using a map and/or written guide provided by the museum. Because this program does not rely on museum staff, large groups of students can often be accommodated. During the self-guided tour, the group's leader, whether chaperon or teacher, often relies upon labels and signs throughout the museum for pertinent information. But self-guided tours can turn into aimless wandering if not well planned. Teachers must establish learning objectives and develop activities to help focus students' attention as they move throughout the museum. When a self-guided tour becomes "self selected," the chaperon and students are not likely to expand their knowledge significantly. Museum visitors who visit museums without a structured program seek out specific experiences and objects that are personally meaningful to them. These experiences only reinforce what they already know. Therefore it is critical that a teacher carefully plan the self-guided tour by setting learning objectives, developing a lesson plan, and preparing the chaperons and the students for their museum visit. For help in planning your self-guided tour, be sure to contact the museum's education department. Many education departments have written materials and a wealth of ideas and experience to assist you in planning self-guided activities.

Student Workshops and Classes for Credit

Student workshops are often several hours long and provide students with the opportunity to study a particular aspect of the museum's collection in depth using a variety of learning techniques and strategies. These workshops may be offered during the school day, after school, and on weekends. Student museum classes for credit are offered by museums in collaboration with the school districts. These student programs are specially designed to meet all the curriculum requirements and are sometimes geared to special needs and gifted students. Typically, such programs cannot accommodate large groups and usually students must meet certain requirements set by the museum to participate in these workshops or classes. Student classes for credit often meet during the regular school day at the museum.

Participatory Galleries and Hands-on Rooms

These special galleries provide students with an abundance of opportunities to examine a variety of collections using all their senses. These galleries are too often mistaken as being appropriate only for young children when in fact they are wonderful learning environments for all ages. School groups must generally reserve a time slot in these galleries during their museum visits.

From *The Field Trip Handbook* by Genean Stec, published by Good Year Books. Copyright © 1992 Chester County Intermediate Unit.

Participatory Activities and Exhibits

In reaching out to new audiences, museums have developed a variety of participatory activities to engage visitors and enrich their museum experiences. These participatory activities help to add another dimension to student learning during a museum visit and can usually be incorporated into a guided or self-guided tour program. Examples of such activities include treasure hunts, drawing and sketching, objective and subjective questions in a worksheet format, writing with a quill pen, drawing water from a well, carding wool, creating a valentine or ornament, or deciphering a radio code.

Participatory exhibits include large-scale models, objects that can be entered such as a model heart or trolley car, computers where visitors can play related games or have particular questions answered, and displays that visitors can manipulate. These participatory exhibits invite museum-goers to use all of their senses.

The information provided in the above descriptions of museum education programs can be used to stimulate discussion and establish a dialogue between teachers and local museum educators. To begin the dialogue call or write a letter to your local museum educator.

In the next section, "Create the Best Field Trip Experience," you will find planning charts and check lists, along with suggestions on ways to prepare your chaperons and students for the forthcoming field trip experience.

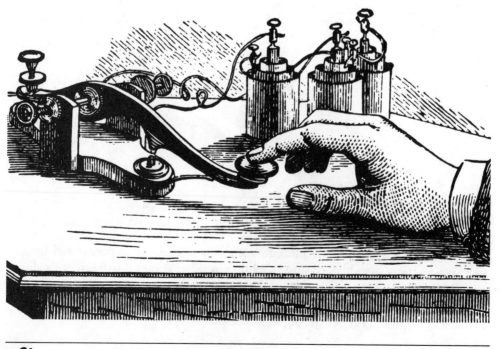

From *The Field Trip Handbook* by Genean Stec, published by Good Year Books. Copyright © 1992 Chester County Intermediate Unit.

Chapter 2
Create the Best Field Trip Experience

Evaluate Past Field Trips

Don't get stuck in a rut. Teachers often return to the same cultural institution year after year with their students. Stop and evaluate the educational experience you and your students receive and compare it to other opportunities offered at other cultural institutions. Use the "Field Trip Survey" worksheet on the following pages to help you conduct your evaluation of past museum experiences. Remember that museums are constantly changing; new exhibitions, new interpretive material, and new educational programs are constantly being developed. Step out of your rut and explore the educational opportunities available at other museums.

Do Some Research

In the early fall, begin to gather information about the cultural institutions in your area. Contact your local chamber of commerce, public library, local tourist information office, county office, or motor club for information about the cultural institutions in the area. Then call or write these institutions and ask for their field trip brochures and/or any information concerning educational resources and opportunities they offer to teachers and students. To help you make these contacts, involve your classroom parent or split the task with another teacher or the school librarian.

As you gather material on local cultural institutions, create a reference file. Encourage the school librarian to create a reference file in the school library on local cultural institutions. Talk to your colleagues about where they have taken their students on field trips and what their experiences have been at different cultural institutions.

From *The Field Trip Handbook* by Genean Stec, published by Good Year Books. Copyright © 1992 Chester County Intermediate Unit.

List Your Choices

When you have collected sufficient information on the cultural institutions in your area, spend time reviewing it and make a list of the institutions and school programs that would enrich areas of your classroom curriculum. Be prepared to make a few phone calls to ask questions you may have concerning particular school programs. Use the worksheet, "Choices and More Choices," in this chapter to help you organize the information you will gather as you peruse the educational material collected from the various museums.

After you have completed your list of appropriate cultural institutions, arrange them in order of relevance to your classroom curriculum. Meet with and talk to all the teachers whose students would participate in the field trip.

Visit Your Choices

Plan a visit to the top three choices on your list to collect more detailed information. If you cannot visit the museums, call their education departments. Use the worksheet, "The Right Fit," in this chapter to help you ask appropriate questions.

If you can visit the museums, call in advance and speak with the staff in the education department. If possible, schedule time to meet with them during your museum planning visit. If you cannot visit all three top choices, split the task with other teachers or your classroom parent. Use the worksheet, "The Right Fit," when you visit the museums to collect information to share with the other teachers before finally deciding on your field trip destination.

The last worksheet in the chapter, "The Final Decision: Why Are We Going to this Museum?", will help you determine which museums to visit with your students.

From *The Field Trip Handbook* by Genean Stec, published by Good Year Books. Copyright © 1992 Chester County Intermediate Unit.

Field Trip Survey: Evaluate Your Past Museum Experiences

Use this worksheet to evaluate your past museum experiences and reasons for participating in field trips. Keep in mind your answers to this evaluation when planning your next field trip.

1. How often are you and your students able to visit museums during the school year?

2. Which are your favorite museums in the area to visit with your students? Why?

3. Describe yourself when you visit a museum *without* your students. (Consider length of time spent, what you look for, use of guides, reading of labels, and so on.)

4. What frustrations have you encountered visiting museums with your students?

5. What exhibitions have you seen that you consider outstanding to visit with students?

6. Describe your school's field trip policy in the following areas:

   a. How many trips are permitted? _____

   b. How many students usually go on a trip? _____

   c. Who decides where to go? _____

   d. Who makes the arrangements? _____

   e. Who pays for the trips? _____

7. What field trips have been the most successful? Why?

8. Any disappointments or disasters on a field trip? Why?

From *The Field Trip Handbook* by Genean Stec, published by Good Year Books. Copyright © 1992 Chester County Intermediate Unit.

9. What kind of preparation do you find most useful to do with your students before a field trip?

10. Have any museums provided you with pre-visit materials? If so, which museums? What do you like about the materials? How have you used the materials with your students?

11. Do you prepare study guides, worksheets, or any other sort of activities for students to use during the field trip? Why or why not?

12. Have you or your students ever been asked to fill out an evaluation form by a museum?

13. How do you evaluate your field trip experiences? Do you have your students evaluate their field trip experiences? Why or why not?

14. Where do you get information about field trips?

15. What are the biggest obstacles to your use of field trips and/or local resources in the classroom?

16. List any field trip ideas you would like to develop but have never tried.

In planning your next field trip, try out a new idea. Talk with the museum educator at the site to help you develop your idea.

From *The Field Trip Handbook* by Genean Stec, published by Good Year Books. Copyright © 1992 Chester County Intermediate Unit.

Choices, and More Choices: Which Museum is Best for My Students?

Make a copy of this form to use with each museum as you gather basic information about the different institutions.

1. Museum:

2. Phone:

3. School Program:

4. Pre- and Post-visit Materials:

5. Curriculum Area of Significance:

6. Cost:

7. Program Limitations (group size, time of day/year offered, skill level of students):

8. Parking:

9. Lunch Facilities:

10. Additional Information:

A more detailed worksheet, "Hold That Date," can be found on page 21. Use it when you have made your final site selection.

From *The Field Trip Handbook* by Genean Stec, published by Good Year Books. Copyright © 1992 Chester County Intermediate Unit.

The Right Fit: Choosing the Museum that Meets the Needs of Your Students

Museums communicate through objects. Visitors come to see these objects, to experience them firsthand. These objects are placed within the context of exhibits. An exhibit acts as a framework to help visitors understand the significance of the objects in relation to themselves and the world. Each exhibit—its colors, lighting, layout, size, and level of sophistication—has been carefully designed to enhance and enrich the visitor's experience with the objects. Exhibits are created to meet the needs of many different audiences. It is important when planning a field trip experience to evaluate the museum and its exhibits for their relevance to your students and their studies.

Use this worksheet during your planning visits to help you evaluate each museum, its exhibits, and its school programs in relation to your students and their educational needs.

1. Make a list of ten phrases or words to describe the physical and emotional characteristics of your students (active, difficulty in focusing, quiet, shy, outgoing, inquisitive, curious, love to participate, eager, hard to manage, polite, disruptive, and so on). Keep these ten characteristics in mind as you review the museum, its school program, and its facilities.

2. Is the museum easy to get to from your school? If not, what special arrangements need to be made to get to the museum?

    Is the museum handicapped accessible?

    Is there bus parking?

    Are there lunch facilities and restrooms?

    Is the museum program weather dependent?

    Does the program take place indoors or out?

3. Does the museum project a welcoming atmosphere? Is the environment appealing or overwhelming to students?

4. When you walk into the museum, what is the first thing you notice?

5. What educational programs and materials does the museum offer for your grade level?

From *The Field Trip Handbook* by Genean Stec, published by Good Year Books. Copyright © 1992 Chester County Intermediate Unit.

6. How long is the program that the students will be involved in at the museum? How is the period of time broken up? Is there a variety of student activities or changes of pace during the time period?

7. What exhibits does the museum's school program use during the field trip experience? Are the students involved in a hands-on activity, a looking activity, or a discussion?

8. What is the theme or topic of this exhibit? Does this have relevance to your students? Why or why not?

9. Can the exhibit comfortably accommodate your group of students?

10. Will your students be the only group using the exhibit at the time of your visit? If not, what other groups will share the exhibit space with you and what are the drawbacks of this situation?

11. Are the labels and signage in the exhibit the appropriate grade-level readability for your students? (This is particularly important if your visit to the museum is self guided because the teacher and chaperon will rely heavily on the information provided in the labels.)

12. Are the objects in the exhibit placed at a level that is comfortable and easy for your students to see?

13. Are there areas throughout the exhibit that will be of particular interest to your students? Make a note of these areas and their locations.

What objects will have particular relevance to your students?

14. What curriculum connections can you make using the exhibit and the objects in the exhibit?

From *The Field Trip Handbook* by Genean Stec, published by Good Year Books. Copyright © 1992 Chester County Intermediate Unit.

List ways to expand and develop ideas touched upon at the museum in relationship to your curriculum.

15. What ideas and information do you think your students will get from the exhibit?

What can you do to ensure that particular information will be absorbed by the students? (List ideas for student activities such as worksheets.)

From *The Field Trip Handbook* by Genean Stec, published by Good Year Books. Copyright © 1992 Chester County Intermediate Unit.

The Final Decision: Why Are We Going to this Museum?

Museum Name _____

1. My educational goals for this field trip and participation in this particular school program are:

    a.

    b.

    c.

2. My learning objectives for this field trip and participation in this particular school program are:

    a.

    b.

    c.

    d.

3. Three curriculum connections are:

    a.

    b.

    c.

4. Ideas for Student Activities:

    a. Pre–Field-Trip Student Activities:

    b. Travel Activities:

    c. Field Trip Student Activities:

    d. Post–Field-Trip Student Activities:

From The Field Trip Handbook by Genean Stec, published by Good Year Books. Copyright © 1992 Chester County Intermediate Unit.

Chapter 3
Plan Your Field Trip

It is important that you begin to plan your field trip well in advance of the actual date. Begin by filling out the school information on the worksheet "Hold That Date" (page 21), including three choices of dates for your visit, and then call or write to the museum. Have the worksheet next to you when scheduling the field trip with the museum staff. After all the arrangements are made, copy the completed worksheet and give it to all the teachers and school personnel involved in the field trip. *It is important that you always make a reservation with the museum even if you and your group will be self-guiding your visit.*

Prepare Your Chaperons

After all the effort you have put forth to engage enough chaperons for your field trip, don't neglect them. Your chaperons are a valuable resource; use them to help make your field trip an educational success. Prepare your chaperons for the trip by sending them a letter or an outline explaining your educational goals and learning objectives for the field trip. Outline the tasks they will be responsible for throughout the day. If possible, prepare a list of the names of the students of whom they will be in charge. If you are all bringing bag lunches, bring along a small treat for your chaperons (candy bars, cans of soda, fancy name tags, or snacks for the ride home). Set aside time to talk with your chaperons and answer their questions before the field trip. Be sure your chaperons know the schedule for the day. Fill out the worksheet "The Field Trip: What Are We Doing Today?" (page 00) for your chaperons to refer to during the trip. When the excursion is over and all are safely back at school, be sure to let your chaperons know how much the school appreciated their participation.

Prepare Your Students

The success of a field trip depends on how well prepared your students are for their visit to the museum. After you have made all the arrangements for field trip day, prepare your students for their museum experience, be it a special program or a self-guided visit. Pre-visit exercises should be both oral and written and should include some hands-on activities. Clarify students' expectations so that you can alleviate unnecessary disappointment. Check with the museum to see if it has any of the following pre-visit materials to use with your students in the classroom:

> *written materials:* vocabulary lists, crossword puzzles, stories, document packets, role-playing activities, background information on specific exhibitions
> *audio visual materials:* films, records, slides, videos

visual materials: posters and pictures that could be used to create a bulletin board display.

An outline for a discussion to help prepare students for a museum field trip can be found on the worksheet on page 25. Chapter Four contains many suggestions and ideas of ways to prepare your students for the field trip. Take the time to peruse this section as you plan the outing.

Students usually cannot leave school grounds during school hours without permission from their parents. Send a copy of the permission form provided in this chapter to each parent or guardian well in advance of the field trip. Be sure that your school district's administrator has authorized your field trip and the day's activities. Review your school district's field trip procedures to ensure that you have met all the requirements concerning safety, parental permission, and legal responsibilities. If there are any special rules or activities related to the field trip, send a copy of them home with each student's permission slip for the parents to review. Remind your students that they must return the signed permission forms in order to participate in the field trip. Post a reminder to the students on the classroom bulletin board.

Discuss Museum Etiquette

Proper behavior on a field trip is important. Review the following museum rules with your students to prepare them for their museum experience. Be sure to explain why it is important to follow each rule.

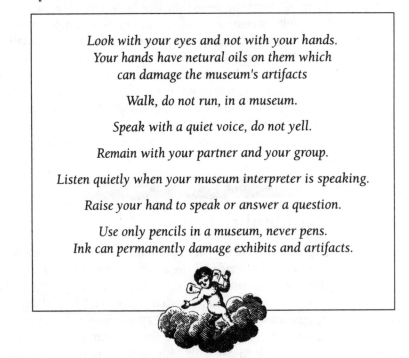

Look with your eyes and not with your hands.
Your hands have netural oils on them which
can damage the museum's artifacts

Walk, do not run, in a museum.

Speak with a quiet voice, do not yell.

Remain with your partner and your group.

Listen quietly when your museum interpreter is speaking.

Raise your hand to speak or answer a question.

Use only pencils in a museum, never pens.
Ink can permanently damage exhibits and artifacts.

Confirm Your Arrangements

The day of the field trip can be very hectic. To help prevent confusion, disappointment, and forgetfulness, use the checklist, "What Have I Forgotten to Do or to Bring?", on page 27 to help you confirm all your arrangements.

From *The Field Trip Handbook* by Genean Stec, published by Good Year Books. Copyright © 1992 Chester County Intermediate Unit.

Hold That Date

Use this form when scheduling your field trip. Share completed copies with teachers and school personnel involved with the trip.

1. Administrative approval of the field trip:

2. Museum:

3. Museum contact person:

4. Phone number:

5. When was the reservation made?

6. School:

7. Address:

8. Phone number:

9. School contact person:

10. Teacher(s) accompanying the group on the field trip:

11. Chaperon(s) accompanying the group on the field trip:

12. Date of field trip: (Have at least three possible dates selected before you call the museum to schedule a field trip.)
    Possible dates:

    a.   b.   c.

13. Time of arrival at the museum:

14. Length of visit:

15. Type of program requested:

    Time of program:

16. Number in group: Cost for each group:

    Number of students: Cost for student:

    Number of teachers/chaperons: Cost for chaperon:

From *The Field Trip Handbook* by Genean Stec, published by Good Year Books. Copyright © 1992 Chester County Intermediate Unit.

Number of bus drivers: Cost for bus driver:

17. Grade level:

18. Subject area:

19. Method of payment:

20. Cancellation policy or rain date:

21. Special arrangements

    Lunch:

    Transportation and parking:

    Handicapped accessibility:

    Type of clothing required (boots, long pants, hat, rain gear, etc.):

    Additional:

22. Transportation arrangements

    Date booked:

    Transportation company:

    Phone:

    Cost: Method of payment:

    Deposit required: Yes/No   Amount: Date due:

    Time of arrival at the school: Time due back at the school:

    Directions to the museum from your school:

Be sure to notify the museum's education department about any self-guided activities or worksheets you have planned for your students during their museum visit. Have extra copies of the activities or worksheets for the museum staff assisting you during your visit.

Request a written field-trip confirmation from the museum and the transportation company.

From *The Field Trip Handbook* by Genean Stec, published by Good Year Books. Copyright © 1992 Chester County Intermediate Unit.

The Field Trip: What Are We Doing Today?

Fill out and distribute this worksheet to your chaperons.

Chaperon: _____

Let me begin by thanking you for participating in this field trip experience. Your assistance is greatly appreciated!

1. The students will be participating in the following museum program(s).

    PROGRAM   TIME

    Tour:

    Workshop:

    Hands-on activity:

    Audiovisual presentation:

2. When and where to meet for lunch

    Time:

    Location:

3. When and where to meet to return to school

    Time:

    Location:

4. Special arrangements:

5. Students are/are not permitted to visit the museum shop.

6. In case of an emergency, contact the museum guards or staff immediately.

From *The Field Trip Handbook* by Genean Stec, published by Good Year Books. Copyright © 1992 Chester County Intermediate Unit.

7. Students you are in charge of today:

   a. _____   g. _____

   b. _____   h. _____

   c. _____   i. _____

   d. _____   j. _____

   e. _____   k. _____

   f. _____   l. _____

8. Review the following rules with your students when you arrive at the museum. Be sure to explain why it is important to follow each rule.

Look with your eyes and not with your hands.
Your hands have netural oils on them which
can damage the museum's artifacts

Walk, do not run, in a museum.

Speak with a quiet voice, do not yell.

Remain with your partner and your group.

Listen quietly when your museum interpreter is speaking.

Raise your hand to speak or answer a question.

Use only pencils in a museum, never pens.
Ink can permanently damage exhibits and artifacts.

From *The Field Trip Handbook* by Genean Stec, published by Good Year Books. Copyright © 1992 Chester County Intermediate Unit.

Preparing for a Field Trip: A Teacher-Student Discussion

Use this outline as a guide when discussing your upcoming field trip with your class.

1. What is a museum?

2. What is the purpose of a museum?

3. Name several different types of museums. How are they similar? How are they different?

4. The museum we will visit on our field trip is:
    What do you think we will see at this museum?
    How many of you (students) have visited this museum before?
    What was your favorite thing in the museum? Why?

5. The reason for our field trip is:

6. During our field trip we will learn about:

7. On our field trip to the museum we will:

    do

    participate in

    tour

    see an audiovisual presentation on

8. On our field trip to the museum we will not:

9. A special part of our museum experience will be:

10. This field trip was planned because it relates to what we are studying in

    (subject or curriculum area).

11. To prepare for our field trip we will:

From *The Field Trip Handbook* by Genean Stec, published by Good Year Books. Copyright © 1992 Chester County Intermediate Unit.

Student Field Trip Permission Form

Parents or guardians of children involved in a field trip should fill this out and return it to the teacher.

Date: _____

I hereby give my child, _____
Name of Student

Permission to go to _____
Name of Museum

And participate in _____

On _____ From _____ To _____
Date   Time   Time

Parent(s) or Guardian(s) Signature(s): _____

_____

Date: _____

Return to school by: _____

_____Yes, I would be available to help chaperon the students on this field trip. Please call

me at _____ with more information concerning the field trip.

_____No, I would not be available to help chaperon the students on this field trip.

- -

Detach and return the above form to school

The cost of the field trip is: _____

This fee includes transportation to and from the site and admission into the site.

Please prepare a bag lunch for your child and include a beverage.

Please dress your child for: _____

The students will/will not be allowed to visit the museum shop.

_____

From *The Field Trip Handbook* by Genean Stec, published by Good Year Books. Copyright © 1992 Chester County Intermediate Unit.

What Have I Forgotten to Do or to Bring?

Hurray, hurray, it's your field-trip day! The following checklist will help you to confirm all the arrangements you have made for the field trip. A quick review of this checklist on the day of your field trip will help prevent confusion, disappointments, and forgetfulness on such a busy day. Review this checklist before you leave your classroom to board your bus.

Museum   Phone Number

_____ A copy of the tour confirmation letter and the day's schedule.

_____ The school phone number.

_____ A map and directions to the museum with information on where to unload the students and where to park.

_____ An accurate head count of the number of students and chaperons with the group.

_____ A list of the students each chaperon will supervise.

_____ Name tags for the students, teachers, and chaperons.

_____ A check or cash for admission and program fees.

_____ Extra coins to make a phone call or for the soda and vending machines.

_____ The student lunches, labeled, collected, and stored in portable containers ready to be loaded on the bus.

_____ Extra lunches for those students, chaperons, and teachers who forgot theirs.

_____ Supplies for museum activities: pencils, paper, clipboards, worksheets.

_____ A camera, film, and a flash to document the students' experiences at the museum. The photographs can be used in post-visit classroom activities. (Be sure to find out if the museum you are visiting allows flash photography. Many don't.)

_____ The number of the bus so it is easy to identify "your" bus at the end of your busy day.

_____ First-aid kit with extra bandages and tissues.

_____ Your student travel activity to occupy students en route to the museum. (See pages 00 and 00 for possible activities.)

_____ Remind students to use the bathrooms *before* boarding the bus.

From *The Field Trip Handbook* by Genean Stec, published by Good Year Books. Copyright © 1992 Chester County Intermediate Unit.

Chapter 4
Student Activities

To be a success, any field trip must be well planned and organized with the students' needs and skills in mind. Remember that monotony brings on boredom and restlessness. Plan your field trip day to include a variety of different activities. Ask yourself: Are the students standing, sitting, walking, listening, speaking, writing, thinking, observing, doing? How long are they doing each activity and in what sequence? Consider rearranging the schedule if it appears that the students will be sitting for long periods of time or walking or listening without a break. Be careful of "information overload." Trying to do too much in one day will result in restlessness and a lack of concentration among students.

Even if you are going to participate in a guided program, you should still prepare a student activity to be done at the museum. This activity could take the form of a worksheet, an observation exercise, a treasure hunt, or many other activities. Design the museum activity to be continued or completed back in the classroom. This will ensure that time is taken to "complete" this educational experience. Be sure to notify the museum's education department about the activity you are planning to do with your students at the museum. If possible, send the staff a copy of the activity or worksheet in advance of your visit.

The following section contains ideas and activities to enrich your field trip experience both in the classroom and in the museum. These activities should be adapted to meet the specific needs and skills of your students and the goals and objectives of your museum visit. They have been arranged under five broad headings—travel, general, art, history, and science. Each student activity page includes a small piece of art near the page number. Travel activity pages show a bus; history activities include a silhouette of an eighteenth-century person; art activities include a framed painting; and science activities show a magnifying glass. Pages for teachers include a small apple and all other pages show a museum building.

From *The Field Trip Handbook* by Genean Stec, published by Good Year Books. Copyright © 1992 Chester County Intermediate Unit.

Many of the activities listed under a particular heading can be adapted for use with other curriculum areas. They range in difficulty from very simple perceptual activities to more complex ones that involve a higher level of thinking skills. These classroom and museum activities will encourage students to describe, compare, contrast, analyze, predict, generalize, abstract, probe, discuss, argue, and think. Students will become involved in object-based learning. These activities will also facilitate the development of language skills as students express their ideas and opinions concerning the objects and experiences they encounter in the museum. To help you in planning activities related to your field trip, review "Pointers on Creating and Conducting Student Activities in Museums" below.

To complete your museum experience it is important to follow it up with a classroom activity. This will help students to summarize their learning and place it into the context of the classroom curriculum. It will also provide the classroom teacher with the opportunity to measure the educational value of the field trip.

Pointers on Creating and Conducting Student Activities in Museums

1. When creating a student activity keep the following points in mind. The activity should:
   a. introduce concepts, ideas, and activities,
   b. stimulate curiosity,
   c. motivate students to ask questions and to participate in discussions, and
   d. review knowledge already acquired.

2. Always use pencils, never pens, when doing activities in museums.

3. If your students are going to be involved in a writing or drawing activity, come prepared with firm writing surfaces such as clipboards or notebooks.

4. Visit the museum and test your student activity before you use it with the entire class. Consider the heights of the objects in the exhibit and the space around the exhibit in relationship to your students. Will the students be able to examine the objects closely and comfortably gather around them to complete the activity?

5. Be aware of "museum fatigue" and "information overload." When testing the activity, time it. Remember, even adults become restless and fatigued after one hour of focused museum learning. Be sure to build in a break or change of pace in planning your student activity.

6. Alert the museum staff before you arrive at the museum that your students will be involved in an activity during their visit. Tell the museum staff which objects or exhibits your students will be using. Always double check with the museum a week before your field trip to be sure that the exhibits and objects you focused on in your activity are available for students to use. Send the museum education staff a copy of your activity.

7. In creating the student activity, develop questions that encourage the students to use their perceptual skills. Create questions that go beyond the information provided in the labels. Develop objective questions and subjective questions

From *The Field Trip Handbook* by Genean Stec, published by Good Year Books. Copyright © 1992 Chester County Intermediate Unit.

that stretch the students' imaginations. Encourage the students to use the information they gather through observation to develop an opinion or point of view concerning an object.

8. If your activity involves a worksheet, provide ample space for the students to write and/or draw and include an extra page. Remember to keep it simple and to minimize the directions.

9. Provide the students with a map of the museum and/or exhibit area where they will do the activity.

10. Review the activity with your students *before* the field trip. Discuss the amount of time the activity will take and other details related to it.

11. Be sure to follow up the student activity. Back in the classroom, take the time to review it. The students should understand the "reason" for the activity. How does the activity relate to the museum experience and their classroom curriculum?

12. Evaluate the success of the student activity. Elicit feedback about it from the students, the chaperons, and the museum staff.

13. Create museum activities for your students based on opportunities for comparison and contrast, questions that will focus the students' attention on the exhibit or a particular artifact, and opportunities for students to interact with one another and to share their opinions, to become involved in the exhibit, and to take the information they have been exposed to and discuss particular ideas with their peers.

From *The Field Trip Handbook* by Genean Stec, published by Good Year Books. Copyright © 1992 Chester County Intermediate Unit.

TRAVELING TO THE MUSEUM

Activities and Worksheets

Traveling to and from the museum can be an enriching experience for the students, and they can spend the time sharpening their observation skills. Carry out the following activities getting there and back.

What Do You See Traveling To and From the Museum?

Design a travel worksheet like the one on page 33 with items for the students to look for along the route to the museum. Before the field trip, get a friend or fellow teacher to drive you along the route so that you can identify an appropriate selection of landmarks and locations for the students to spot. You might ask: "How many _____ did you see on your way to the museum?" The blank might be trains, bridges, lakes, rivers, oceans, cornfields, wheatfields, tractors, parks, fast-food places, churches, schools, dogs, gas stations, police officers, cement trucks, yellow houses, and so on.

Mind Teasers

Word games are good to play on the way back to school as a review of new vocabulary terms learned that day at the museum. Develop crossword puzzles, word searches, and word scrambles using vocabulary related to the field trip experience. To prepare this activity, talk with the museum education staff to get a list of such terms.

Connect the Dots

Project the image of an object, the museum's logo, or something of significance to the field trip experience on the wall. Using its silhouette, create a connect-the-dot exercise for the students to complete as they travel to the museum.

Sing-Along

Meet with the music teacher and find out if there are any simple songs related to the topic or theme of your field trip. Learn them and ask the music teacher to teach them to the students. Print up sheets with the words on them to hand out to the chaperons and students. Sing the songs together on the bus.

Riddles and Clues

Create a riddle related to the field trip for each student to solve as you travel to the museum.

From *The Field Trip Handbook* by Genean Stec, published by Good Year Books. Copyright © 1992 Chester County Intermediate Unit.

Name _____ Date _____

Transportation Tally

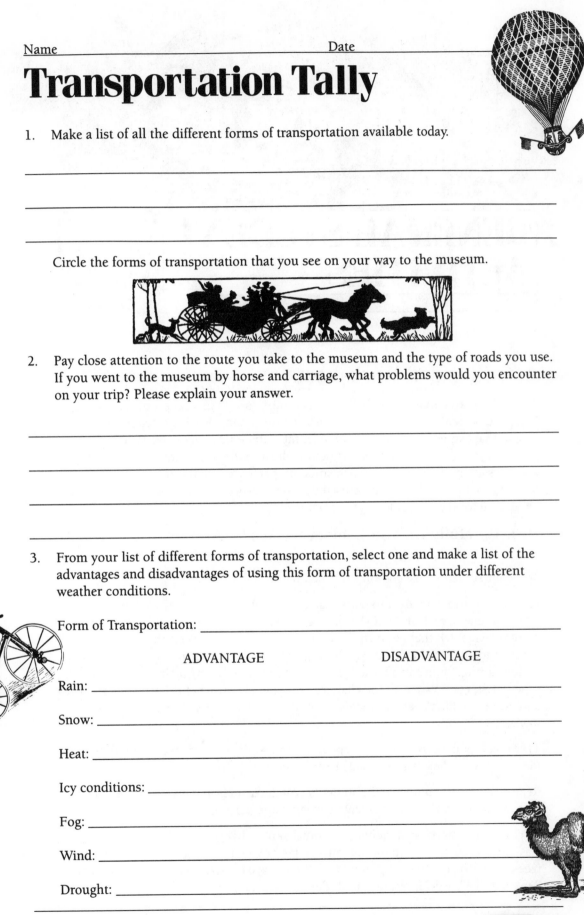

1. Make a list of all the different forms of transportation available today.

_____

_____

_____

Circle the forms of transportation that you see on your way to the museum.

2. Pay close attention to the route you take to the museum and the type of roads you use. If you went to the museum by horse and carriage, what problems would you encounter on your trip? Please explain your answer.

_____

_____

_____

_____

3. From your list of different forms of transportation, select one and make a list of the advantages and disadvantages of using this form of transportation under different weather conditions.

Form of Transportation: _____

ADVANTAGE   DISADVANTAGE

Rain: _____

Snow: _____

Heat: _____

Icy conditions: _____

Fog: _____

Wind: _____

Drought: _____

GENERAL STUDENT ACTIVITIES

Activities and Worksheets

These General Activities and Worksheets can be used in any museum setting. Designed for students of various ages and abilities, they provide teachers with a format that can be easily adapted to meet their students' special needs. These activities can be used with students before, during, and after a museum visit. The activities are meant to help sharpen students' perceptual skills and enrich the learning that takes place at the museum, and are especially helpful for those visiting a museum for the first time or are self-guided.

How Carefully Do You Look at the World Around You? (Pre-visit Activity)

Test your students' observation skills before they take a field trip.

Have the students divide into pairs. Each pair should stand facing each other. Upon your command, each student should look carefully at the other student for thirty seconds. Then tell them to turn their backs to one another. With their backs to each other, students should change something about their person (push their sleeves up, remove a ring, unbutton a button, take off their earrings, put their watch on the other wrist, etc.). When all the changes are complete, instruct the students to turn and face each other again. Students must try to guess what changes their partners made.

Take a poll of the class. How perceptive are the students? How many students identified what their partners had changed on their first guess?

Repeat the activity but have the students switch partners and give them less time to study each other. Have the students become more perceptive?

To continue to develop students' perceptual skills, change something in the classroom each day before the students arrive or when they are out for lunch or at recess. Challenge them to figure out what you have changed. Give a "Perceptive Person of the Week" award to the student(s) who are alert to the changes you make.

From *The Field Trip Handbook* by Genean Stec, published by Good Year Books. Copyright © 1992 Chester County Intermediate Unit.

What Is It? (Pre-visit Activity)

Bring in an object from your home, something students would not recognize immediately. Look in your basement, attic, or grandmother's garage. Place the object on a table where the students can come up and see it. Instruct the students not to talk about the object to each other. After all the students have had an opportunity to examine the object, ask each student to write down on a piece of paper what he or she thinks it is. (By writing their guesses students can remain anonymous and will not be afraid that their ideas are silly or wrong.) Collect their answers and review them. Then share the ideas with the entire class. Do not reveal what the object is. Ask the students questions and give them a few clues that will help them identify the object. Let them "work" at figuring out how it is or was used. Encourage students to be creative when thinking about the name and function of the object. This activity can be done verbally with students too young to write.

As a continuation of the activity, challenge students to bring in a mystery object for their classmates to puzzle over.

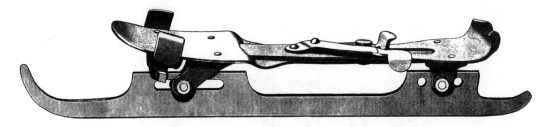

101 Observations (Pre-visit or Museum Activity)

To sharpen students' observation skills, select a very common everyday object or a "mystery" object (something students would not immediately recognize) and pass it around the class. As each student receives this object he or she must make one observation about it. Observations cannot be repeated. The last few students to examine the object will have a more difficult time making observations; be prepared to give them some encouragement. Students might observe that the object is heavy, the object is made from ____, the object smells like ____, the object is ____ in color, the object could be used for ____, and so on.

As each student makes an observation, comment on how that observation may reflect the object's purpose or physical make-up; current technology; the social values of the society; the trends, fads, fashion, or environmental concerns of the time period; or anything else of relevance. This activity will encourage students to look closely at the object for information. Emphasize that even if you don't know what an object is, careful observation can reveal a great deal about it and enable you to make an educated guess about its purpose.

This activity can also be done in a museum using objects in an exhibit or collection. It will help students to spend time *looking* at the objects. Visitor studies conducted by museums note that the average museum visitor spends less than ten seconds looking at an object. How can one possibly learn anything about an object in such little time? This activity will help to focus students' attention and encourage observations.

A Shadow of Doubt (Pre-visit Activity)

What can you learn from a shadow? Create a screen with a large piece of white paper or an old sheet and put a bright light behind it. Collect several common objects of odd shapes and sizes. Have a student sit behind the screen and hold an object up in front of the light. Ask the class to guess what it is by looking at its shadow. Discuss with the class what you can learn about this object by looking at its shadow. Make a list of the object's characteristics. Try to stump the students by holding the object sideways or upside down.

Word Mania (Pre-visit or Post-visit Activity)

This activity can be done to introduce the field trip experience or to provide a review of the museum experience.

Contact the museum educator to get a list of vocabulary words related to the museum experience. Create word jumbles, word searches, matching exercises, or spelling bees using the special vocabulary terms. Discuss the definition and purpose of each new term with the students. After they complete the word games, review the exercises and the definitions with them. If the word games are used in a post-visit activity, ask the students when each word was used during their field trip experience.

Questions, Questions, and More Questions (Pre-visit Activity)

Asking questions is an important skill all students should develop. Museums offer students an ideal environment to develop this language arts skill. By asking questions about an object a student becomes involved with that object, questions lead to answers, which lead to more questions, and the circle of learning continues. Select an object—it can be a common object such as a desk, backpack, pencil, and so on. Place it where all the students can see it. Ask each student to write three questions related to the object. Instruct the students to write one objective question and two subjective questions.

Then have the students share their questions with the rest of the class. Answer the questions as a group. List all the answers on the chalkboard. Finally, discuss with the students what you all have learned about the object.

Stretch the Imagination to Create a New Tool (Pre-visit Activity)

Select a common object and ask the students to pretend they are inventors. As inventors they must each come up with three new uses for this common object. A pencil, for instance, might become a pointer, a back scratcher, or a knitting needle.

From *The Field Trip Handbook* by Genean Stec, published by Good Year Books. Copyright © 1992 Chester County Intermediate Unit.

Which One Is It? (Pre-visit Activity)

Select three to five similar objects, such as coffee mugs, spoons with different handles, books, pens, or pencils. Put one object in a bag or box and have a student, without looking, examine the object by touching it. Then line up all the similar objects and see if the students can select the one they examined by touch.

Set up several stations in the classroom. Have the students work in pairs and move from station to station.

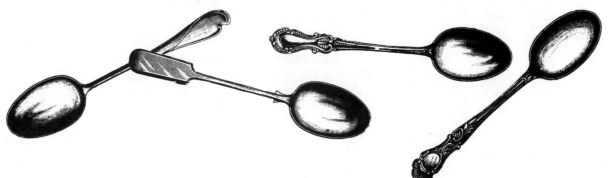

To Know By Touch (Pre-visit Activity)

This activity uses the sense of touch. Place an object in a bag or box. Have the students take turns reaching into the bag or box to feel the object. Then have them write a description of the object and what they think it is. The students should share their descriptions with each other and their ideas on what the object is. Uncover the object and discuss with the students what characteristics they missed because they could not see the object and what characteristics stood out because they had to rely on the sense of touch. Suggestions for objects include kitchen, garden, and carpentry tools; office equipment such as a staple remover; or parts of a larger object such as a vacuum attachment. Try to select an object made from several different types of materials.

Detail, Details, and More Details (Pre-visit Activity)

To sharpen students' descriptive skills, have them make lists of fifteen adjectives describing objects that they can see from their desks. Have each student read his or her adjectives aloud to see if classmates can guess what is being described. Be sure to remind the students not to give away their objects by constantly looking at or pointing to them.

What Do You Know and What Did You Learn? (Pre-visit and Post-visit Activity)

To introduce the field trip topic and determine what the students know about it, write the topic in the middle of the blackboard. Invite the students to tell you all the words and ideas they know related to this topic. Jot down all their suggestions even if they are wrong. Ask each student to copy the list onto paper and to put his or her name on it. Collect the papers.

Repeat the exercise after the field trip experience. This will help the students recall what they learned. Hand out the lists that they made before the excursion. Compare the lists. Discuss with the students what new things they learned about the topic and which of their ideas changed. Have the students cross out any misinformation on the pre-visit list.

niddy noddy

SPECIES

chiaroscuro

Expanding My Vocabulary (Post-visit Activity)

To review the field trip experience back in the classroom, have the students create a list of new vocabulary words they encountered during the trip. Write the list on the blackboard and have the students copy it onto paper. Discuss each word:

What does the word mean?

How was it used during the field trip?

Why is it important?

Instruct each student to select five words from the list of new vocabulary terms and use them in a short paragraph describing the field trip experience.

The Most Important Thing I Learned on My Field Trip (Post-visit Activity)

Back in the classroom after the field trip, ask each student to write a short paragraph on the most important thing he or she learned during the experience, giving two reasons why it is important.

From *The Field Trip Handbook* by Genean Stec, published by Good Year Books. Copyright © 1992 Chester County Intermediate Unit.

I Would Like To Introduce . . . (Post-visit Activity)

Back in the classroom after the field trip, ask each student to select an artist, historical figure, or scientist he or she learned about during the outing. Tell the students that they have been asked to introduce this person to their classmates. Have the students list three important things they would say about this person. Then have the students take turns pretending to introduce their selected people to their classmates. To help the students overcome any fear of speaking aloud, set an example by doing the activity yourself.

Expressing My Opinion (Post-visit activity)

When you return to the classroom, ask the students to write a short essay on what they liked most about their field trip experience and what they liked least. Instruct the students to give at least two reasons to support their likes and dislikes.

It's the Greatest (Post-visit Activity)

After the field trip, ask students to select an object that they saw during the trip and create an advertisement to sell this great object. To help the students create their ads use the worksheet on page 41.

My Favorite Thing at the Museum was . . . (Post-visit Activity)

Discuss with your students the high points of their field trip day. What did they like the best? What did they like the least? What new fact or piece of information did they learn during the experience? How does it help them in their studies? Ask them why they think you planned this particular field trip for them. How did the field trip relate to what they are studying in the classroom?

From *The Field Trip Handbook* by Genean Stec, published by Good Year Books. Copyright © 1992 Chester County Intermediate Unit.

Write All About It (Post-visit Activity)

Have students write thank-you letters to the museum telling what impressed them the most and what they learned during the field trip experience. To really challenge students, have them create poems reflecting their feelings about the field trip. Have younger students draw pictures to reflect the experience.

Headline News: Students Visit the _____ Museum! (Post-visit Activity)

Have the students pretend they are newspaper journalists reporting on the events of their field trip. Divide the students into groups to write on various topics such as the route to the museum, hands-on experiences in the museum, the lunchtime adventures, the missing _____, ten most interesting facts about _____, and so on. Share the newspaper articles with other students, parents, and the museum staff.

Movie Time (Post-visit Activity)

Show the students a film, filmstrip, or video on a topic related to their museum visit. Ask them which they enjoyed more—seeing the film or visiting the museum. Have them explain their answers.

Read All About It! (Post-visit Activity)

Ask your school librarian to create a bibliography of books related to the topic of your field trip experience. The list could include fiction, nonfiction, biographies and autobiographies about artists, historians, scientists, and historic or scientific events touched upon during your trip. After the field trip, visit the school library with your students and help them select books to read from this special bibliography. After they have read the books, have the students present oral reports to their classmates sharing particular information that relates back to their field trip experience.

From *The Field Trip Handbook* by Genean Stec, published by Good Year Books. Copyright © 1992 Chester County Intermediate Unit.

It's the Greatest

The Object is: _____

1. Five unusual features of this object are:

   a. _____

   b. _____

   c. _____

   d. _____

   e. _____

2. You must buy this object because it will

   _____

   _____

3. This object will make your life

   _____

   _____

4. Draw a picture of this object.

5. Create your advertisement.
   Remember, you want to catch people's attention.
   Use bright colors and bold words.

From *The Field Trip Handbook* by Genean Stec, published by Good Year Books. Copyright © 1992 Chester County Intermediate Unit.

Activities and Worksheets

Art is a form of communication. An artist skillfully orders various materials to communicate a human experience. To understand and appreciate art one must become familiar with its basic elements—line, color, shape, and texture. These elements are the tools the artist uses to create a unique arrangement.

> *Color* is a critical element in the creation of two-dimensional art. No form can be seen unless it is placed against a different color. Color is also used by an artist to communicate feeling.

> *Line* is a mark that connects two points. It can be used to express ideas and feelings. It can also be used in a painting to lead the eye from one part of the painting to another.

> *Shape,* or form, is defined by the area containing color. People and things have shapes. In different cultures certain shapes are recognized as having particular meanings, such as the octagon of a stop sign or the silhouette of a person.

> *Texture* is the tactile quality of a surface or the representation of that surface. It is the way something feels when you touch it. In a painting, texture is what your eyes tell you about how things in the painting would feel if you could touch them.

The following activities will help students become familiar with the elements of art and develop understanding and appreciation of art. They will also enhance the art museum field trip experience.

Art Puzzles (Pre-visit and Museum Activity)

Collect a selection of postcards or small prints of the artworks that students will see on their field trip to the art museum. Cut up the postcards or small prints into different shapes. Put them in envelopes. Give each student an envelope of art puzzles pieces to put together. Each student will have a special work of art to look for during the field trip.

From *The Field Trip Handbook* by Genean Stec, published by Good Year Books. Copyright © 1992 Chester County Intermediate Unit.

Illustrating Words (Pre-visit, Museum, and Post-visit Activity)

Before your field trip, visit the art museum to familiarize yourself with its exhibits. Select an exhibit and create a list of topics related to it. In the classroom, have the students select topics from your list and write stories related to the topic. Have the students pretend that their stories are to be published and that they must select artists and works of art to illustrate their stories. During their field trip to the museum, allow students to tour the selected exhibit with their chaperons to "select" their artists and works of art. Instruct the students to record the artist's name, title of the work, and a brief description and sketch. In the classroom, have the students share their selections with the class and briefly explain why they chose those particular artists and works of art to illustrate their stories.

Color Alert! (Pre-visit and Museum Activity)

Ask the students to name their favorite colors and why. Discuss with the students the "character" of colors. What color makes you feel happy, sad, peaceful, angry, warm, cool, hot, cold, calm, restless, sleepy, or lively?

Collect swatches of colors in a large bag or box. The color swatches can be of fabric or paper. Have each student choose a color swatch and glue it to a piece of paper. Instruct them to walk around the school yard and building and make a list of where they see their colors. Was the color a part of a human-made object or was it part of nature?

When the students go on their field trip to the art museum have them take along their color swatches. Have the students make lists of how many different ways their colors are used in the art works they see.

Shape Alert! (Pre-visit and Museum Activity)

Do the Color Alert student activity using shapes such as triangles, squares, rectangles, ovals, circles, and so on.

Color Day (Pre-visit Activity)

Each week have an official "Color Day." Have the students select a color to wear on Color Day. On the chalkboard, make two lists of where you find that color in nature and in the human-made environment. Discuss the character of the color with the students. How does the color make them feel?

Shaping the Landscape (Pre-visit Activity)

This activity will sharpen students' observation skills and stretch their imaginations. Cut shapes out of the center of landscape prints or illustrations (use old magazines books, postcards, and prints). Save the originals to use later. Give each student a

From *The Field Trip Handbook* by Genean Stec, published by Good Year Books. Copyright © 1992 Chester County Intermediate Unit.

shape and have them glue it to a large piece of paper. Have the students create landscapes around their shapes expanding any buildings or natural features depicted in them such as fences, trees, hills, and so on. After the students have completed their landscapes, they should compare them to the originals. How are they similar? How are they different? What features do they have in common?

Creating a Portrait (Pre-visit Activity)

The preceding activity can also be done using portraits. Collect portraits of people and cut out a prominent feature from each. Have each student create a portrait using a cut out. When the students have completed their portraits, ask each to describe the character or personality of the person he or she created and what inspired that conclusion.

Compare and Contrast (Pre-visit or Museum Activity)

This student activity can be done in the classroom or in the museum by a group or individuals using the worksheet on page 49. In the classroom, use large reproductions of artworks or slides to do the activity.

Getting to Know an Artist (Pre-visit, Museum, and Post-visit Activity)

Pre-visit component
Before you take your field trip to the art museum, have each student select an artist whose works you will see during the visit. Ask the museum to send you background information on the artists' lives and artistic styles. Some museum education departments have catalogs and books that they are willing to lend to teachers. Provide an opportunity for the students to browse through the materials provided by the museum or to use the encyclopedia in your school library to collect some basic information on the artists they selected.

Have each student record ten facts about the artist and his or her artistic style.

Museum component
At the museum, allow the students an opportunity to find artwork(s) by the artists they selected. Have the students select one artwork and record ten prominent features of it. Remind them to look at the artist's use of color, line, shape, texture, and subject matter. If a museum guide is working with your students during their visit, allow the students an opportunity to ask the guide questions about their artists.

Post-visit component
Back in the classroom, have the students use all the information they gathered to write short biographies on their artists. Have the students share their biographies with their classmates.

Use the worksheet on page 51 to help the students collect and organize the information.

From *The Field Trip Handbook* by Genean Stec, published by Good Year Books. Copyright © 1992 Chester County Intermediate Unit.

Clues (Museum and Post-visit Activity)

From the museum's education department or shop obtain a selection of postcards or small prints of the art students will see during their visit. Cut out a piece of each postcard or print (choose a "clue" to the painting such as a small object found in the painting, a piece of clothing, a building, an animal, and so on) and glue this clue to a piece of cardboard about six inches square. Give each student a piece of cardboard with a clue. As "art detectives," the students will look for the paintings that match their visual clues.

Have each student record the name of his or her painting and briefly describe it on the back of the cardboard. Back in the classroom, ask students to share their findings with classmates.

This activity can also be done using written clues. Give each student a short description of some part of a particular work of art that the group will see during the museum visit.

The Interview (Museum and Post-visit Activity)

Museum component
At the art museum, have each student select an artwork with a person in it. It can be a landscape, a portrait, or a sculpture. Have students pretend to interview the people in their artworks. Who are they? What are they doing? Where are they going? Why are they dressed the way they are?

Post-visit component
Using the answers to the above questions as a starting point, in the classroom have the students write short stories about the adventures of the people they interviewed.

Favorites (Museum and Post-visit Activity)

Museum component
This activity can be done as a group discussion or as a quiet writing activity. As a wrap-up activity at the museum, ask your students which artworks are their favorites and which are their least favorites. Have the students list at least five reasons to explain their choices.

Post-visit component
Back in the classroom, have the students write short essays about their visit discussing their favorite and least favorite artworks at the museum. Allow the students to use the lists they created at the museum to help them write their essays.

From *The Field Trip Handbook* by Genean Stec, published by Good Year Books. Copyright © 1992 Chester County Intermediate Unit.

First Prize! (Museum and Post-visit Activity)

Museum component
Print each of the following terms on separate index cards: line, color, shape, and texture. At the museum, divide the students into small teams of three and four. Give each team a card with a word on it. Members of each team are to pretend that they are judges for a county art show. Each team of judges must jointly select the work of art that it feels should receive first prize for the term on its card. Each team should list five reasons for its choice. Have the students share their selections and reasons with their classmates.

Post-visit component
Back in the classroom, ask students to pretend again that they are judges for the county art show. The county newspaper has asked the judges to write a short article on the art show giving their overall impression of all the works of art and then singling out for discussion the artworks they selected as their first-prize winners. Remind the students to refer to their lists of five reasons to help them write their essays.

Can You Sit Still? (Museum Activity)

To encourage students to look more carefully at the composition, or the arrangement, of a work of art, select a work with several figures in it. Instruct the students to copy the poses of the figures. Ask the students why the artist might have chosen to arrange the figures in those poses. How would students change the poses of the figures? How would that change the impact of the artwork?

Poetry Inspired by Art (Museum and Post-visit Activity)

Museum component
At the museum, ask the students to select works of art that they like. Have each student sit or stand in front of the chosen artwork and complete the worksheet on page 53.

Post-visit component
Back in the classroom, have the students use their worksheets to help them create simple poems using similes or metaphors. Complete the activity by reading the poems aloud in the classroom. Create a bulletin board display using the students' poems and pictures of the related artworks. Use postcard illustrations or small prints acquired from the museum or ask the students to draw pictures of their artworks for the bulletin board.

How Carefully Do You Observe? (Pre-visit or Museum Activity)

This worksheet activity is best done in the museum, though it can be done in the classroom using large reproductions or slides of artworks. It can be done as a group activity or individually. Six worksheets (see pages 55–65) correspond to the six different types of paintings to be found in most museums—landscape, portrait, still life, genre, narrative, and non-objective/abstract.

Once Upon a Time (Museum or Post-visit Activity)

The student worksheet on page 66 is designed as a creative writing activity. Ideally, it should be done at the art museum in front of the original works of art that the students select to write about, but it is more practical to do it in the classroom after the field trip. If you do it in the classroom, be sure the students see the original works of art at the museum during their visit and then provide postcards, reproductions, posters, or slides of the works they selected. If you do it at the museum, students will need a sturdy writing surface such as a clipboard or notebook and a pencil. This activity will take a fair amount of time to complete, so inform the students that they may sit on the floor in front of their chosen artworks. Many museums have portable stools to use in the exhibits. Ask the museum education staff if you may use them for this activity.

From *The Field Trip Handbook* by Genean Stec, published by Good Year Books. Copyright © 1992 Chester County Intermediate Unit.

Compare and Contrast

Compare and contrast the work of art by _____

to the work of art by _____.

In following five categories list three ways the works of art are similar and three ways they are different in terms of color, line, shape, texture, and subject matter.

SIMILAR   DIFFERENT

Color:

1. _____

2. _____

3. _____

Line:

1. _____

2. _____

3. _____

Shape:

1. _____

2. _____

3. _____

Texture:

1. _____

2. _____

3. _____

Subject matter:

1. _____

2. _____

3. _____

List and explain two ways the artworks are similar and two ways they are different in terms of the emotions they evoke.

SIMILAR   DIFFERENT

1. _____

2. _____

After comparing and contrasting these two artworks, which do you like the best? Give two reasons for your answer.

_____

_____

_____

From *The Field Trip Handbook* by Genean Stec, published by Good Year Books. Copyright © 1992 Chester County Intermediate Unit.

Name _____ Date _____ *Picasso*

Getting to Know an Artist

The Artist: _____

List ten facts about the artist and his or her artistic style.

1. _____

2. _____

3. _____

4. _____

5. _____

6. _____

7. _____

8. _____

9. _____

10. _____

At the museum, select a work by the artist.

Title: _____

Date: _____

From *The Field Trip Handbook* by Genean Stec, published by Good Year Books. Copyright © 1992 Chester County Intermediate Unit.

Henry Moore

Matisse

Vincent

Klee

List ten prominent features of the artwork that reflect the artist's style.

1. _____

2. _____

3. _____

4. _____

5. _____

6. _____

7. _____

8. _____

9. _____

10. _____

Back in the classroom, write a short biography of the artist describing his or her artistic style and the type of art he or she produced.

Reflect and write about why you like or do not like the work of this artist.

_____

_____

_____

_____

_____

_____

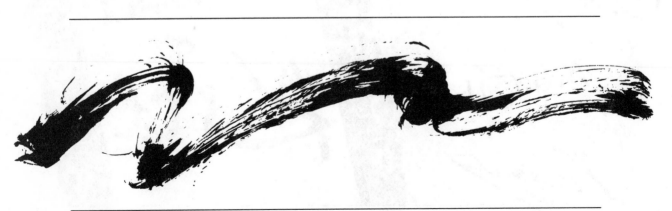

_____

From *The Field Trip Handbook* by Genean Stec, published by Good Year Books. Copyright © 1992 Chester County Intermediate Unit.

Name _____ Date _____

Poetry Inspired by Art

The work of art I selected is called _____

and was created by _____.

Draw a sketch of the work of art.

List ten adjectives that describe the painting or sculpture. Remember to look closely at how the artist used color, line, shape, texture, and subject matter.

1. _____   6. _____

2. _____   7. _____

3. _____   8. _____

4. _____   9. _____

5. _____   10. _____

List five things this artwork reminds you of.

1. _____

2. _____

3. _____

4. _____

5. _____

List five things or characteristics that are opposite those seen in the artwork.

1. _____

2. _____

3. _____

4. _____

5. _____

List three words that describe how this painting makes you feel.

1. _____   3. _____

2. _____

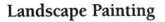

How Carefully Do You Observe?

Landscape Painting

Landscape: A depiction of the out-of-doors

Carefully study the painting by _____
for one minute. Now turn away and answer the following questions.

1. Are there any people depicted in this painting? If so, how many are there and where are they located? Describe what they are wearing.

    _____

    _____

    _____

    _____

2. Describe what the people are doing.

    _____

    _____

    _____

3. Are there any buildings in the painting? If so, where are they located?

    _____

    _____

    _____

4. What time of day is it? _____

5. Describe the weather conditions. _____

6. What season is it? _____

From *The Field Trip Handbook* by Genean Stec, published by Good Year Books. Copyright © 1992 Chester County Intermediate Unit.

7. How much of the painting is covered by open space such as fields or meadows?

_____

How much of the painting is covered by forests?

_____

How much of the painting is covered by water in a lake, pond, ocean, or river?

_____

How much of the painting is covered by the sky?

_____

8. Describe the kind of brush strokes used to create this painting.

_____

9. Describe the surface of the painting. Is it smooth or rough?

_____

10. Describe the sense of depth in the painting. Does it feel like you could walk into the painting?

_____

11. Did the artist sign the painting? If so, how and where did the artist sign his or her name?

_____

When you have completed the questions, face the painting and check your answers. How many did you answer correctly and completely? Rate your observation skills on the scale below.

	1	2	3	4	5
	poor		average		good

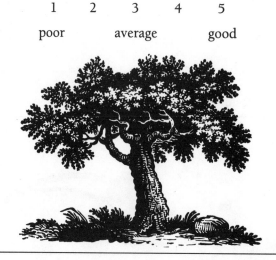

From *The Field Trip Handbook* by Genean Stec, published by Good Year Books. Copyright © 1992 Chester County Intermediate Unit.

How Carefully Do You Observe?

Portrait Painting

Portrait: A depiction of an individual or group of individuals

Carefully study the painting by _____
for one minute. Now turn away and answer the following questions.

1. Briefly describe the "character" of the figure(s) in this portrait. Are they serious, gloomy, cheerful, etc.?

    _____

    _____

2. Describe the figure's clothing.

    _____

    _____

    _____

    Is the figure wearing a hat? _____

3. Is the figure holding anything in his or her hands?

    _____

    _____

4. Describe the background around the figure. Is the figure inside or outside?

_____

_____

5. What other objects are depicted in the painting?

_____

_____

6. Describe the kind of brush strokes used to create the painting.

_____

7. Describe the surface of the painting. Is it smooth or rough?

_____

8. Did the artist sign the painting? If so, how and where did the artist sign his or her name?

_____

When you have completed the questions, face the painting and check your answers. How many did you answer correctly and completely? Rate your observation skills on the scale below.

 1   2   3   4   5
poor   average   good

From *The Field Trip Handbook* by Genean Stec, published by Good Year Books. Copyright © 1992 Chester County Intermediate Unit.

From *The Field Trip Handbook* by Genean Stec, published by Good Year Books. Copyright © 1992 Chester County Intermediate Unit.

Name_____ Date _____

How Carefully Do You Observe?

Still-Life Painting

Still Life: A depiction of objects such as fruit, flowers, kitchen utensils, and so on arranged in a particular way

Carefully study the painting by _____
for one minute. Now turn away and answer the following questions.

1. How many objects are represented in the painting? _____

    Name all the objects depicted in the painting.

    _____

    _____

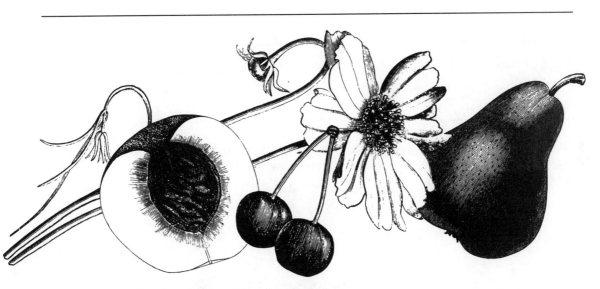

2. Where are the objects located?

3. What are the most prominent colors in the painting?

    _____

4. What is in the center of the painting?

    _____

5. Describe the background in the painting.

    _____

    _____

6. Is there a sense of depth in the painting? Do you feel as if you could reach into the painting and touch the objects? Why or why not?

_____

_____

7. Describe the kind of brush strokes used to create the painting.

_____

8. Describe the surface of the painting. Is it smooth or rough?

_____

9. Is the source of light in the painting natural (sun or moon) or artificial (candles, lamps, etc.).

_____

10. From what direction does the source of light come in the painting? Do the objects in the painting cast shadows?

_____

11. Did the artist sign the painting? If so, how and where did the artist sign his or her name?

_____

When you have completed the questions, face the painting and check your answers. How many did you answer correctly and completely? Rate your observation skills on the scale below.

1   2   3   4   5

poor   average   good

From *The Field Trip Handbook* by Genean Stec, published by Good Year Books. Copyright © 1992 Chester County Intermediate Unit.

How Carefully Do You Observe?

Genre Scene

Genre Scene: A depiction of everyday life

Carefully study the painting by _____
for one minute. Now turn away and answer the following questions.

1. Describe what is going on in the painting.

_____

_____

Are there any people in the painting? If so, what are they doing?

_____

_____

Are there any buildings in the painting? Is so, what kind of buildings are they?

_____

_____

2. Where does this scene take place?

Is it inside or outside? _____

Is it in the country or in the city? _____

_____

From *The Field Trip Handbook* by Genean Stec, published by Good Year Books. Copyright © 1992 Chester County Intermediate Unit.

3. What are the most prominent colors in the painting? _____

_____

4. What is in the center of the painting? _____

_____

5. What time of day is it? _____

 What season is it? _____

6. Describe the weather conditions. _____

7. Is there a sense of depth in this painting? Does it feel as if you could step into the scene? Why or why not?

_____

_____

8. Describe the kind of brush strokes used to create the painting.

_____

9. Describe the surface of the painting. Is it smooth or rough?

_____

10. Did the artist sign the painting? If so, how and where did the artist sign his or her name?

_____

When you have completed the questions, face the painting and check your answers. How many did you answer correctly and completely? Rate your observation skills on the scale below.

1   2   3   4   5

poor   average   good

From *The Field Trip Handbook* by Genean Stec, published by Good Year Books. Copyright © 1992 Chester County Intermediate Unit.

How Carefully Do You Observe?

Narrative Painting

Narrative Painting: A depiction of a historical, biblical, or mythological event

Carefully study the painting by _____
for one minute. Now turn away and answer the following questions.

1. What historical, biblical, or mythological event is being depicted? If you do not know, describe what is happening in the scene.

_____

_____

Are there any people in the painting? If so, what are they doing?

_____

_____

Are there any buildings in the painting? If so, describe the buildings.

_____

_____

2. Where does this scene take place? _____

    Is it inside or outside? _____

    Is it in the country or in the city? _____

3. What are the most prominent colors in the painting? _____

_____

_____

From *The Field Trip Handbook* by Genean Stec, published by Good Year Books. Copyright © 1992 Chester County Intermediate Unit.

4. What is in the center of the painting? _____

_____

5. What time of day is it? _____

What season is it? _____

6. Describe the kind of brush strokes used to create the painting.

_____

7. Describe the surface of the painting. Is it smooth or rough?

_____

8. Did the artist sign the painting? If so, how and where did the artist sign his or her name?

_____

When you have completed the questions, face the painting and check your answers. How many did you answer correctly and completely? Rate your observation skills on the scale below.

1	2	3	4	5
poor		average		good

From *The Field Trip Handbook* by Genean Stec, published by Good Year Books. Copyright © 1992 Chester County Intermediate Unit.

Name _____ Date _____

How Carefully Do You Observe?

Non-Objective/Abstract Work

Non-Objective/Abstract Work: An artistic creation using the elements of art— color, line, shape, and texture—with no recognizable subject matter

Carefully study the painting or work of art by _____
for one minute. Now turn away and answer the following questions.

1. Describe the most prominent colors in this work of art.

    _____

2. Describe the most prominent shapes in this work of art.

    _____

3. What is in the center of the work?

    _____

4. Describe the kind of brush strokes used to create this work.

    _____

5. Describe the surface of the work. Is it smooth or rough?

    _____

6. Are there any other materials used to create the work besides paint?

    _____

7. Describe the sense of depth in the work.

    _____

8. Did the artist sign the work. If so, how and where did the artist sign his or her name?

    _____

When you have completed the questions, face the painting and check your answers. How many did you answer correctly and completely? Rate your observation skills on the scale below.

    1   2   3   4   5
  poor   average   good

_____

 65

Once Upon a Time

Pretend you are a writer for the school newspaper. Your assignment is to write a humorous short story about the summer adventures of a student or teacher in your school. Select one work of art in the museum to illustrate an event, person, or place in your story. Find a comfortable spot from which you can see the artwork you have selected and do your writing. Be sure to refer to things or events depicted in the painting in your story.

In the space below list the name of the work of art and the artist. Briefly describe the work of art and the reasons you chose it as an illustration for your short story. Be sure to describe how the person(s), place, or thing(s) in this work of art illustrate your short story.

Title of the artwork: _____

Artist: _____

nce _____

_____

_____

_____

_____

_____

_____

_____

_____

_____

_____

_____

The End.

From *The Field Trip Handbook* by Genean Stec, published by Good Year Books. Copyright © 1992 Chester County Intermediate Unit.

Activities and Worksheets

For many students history is the memorization of names, dates, and events from the past which seem to have no bearing on their lives today. Museums can help teachers by capturing a student's interest and curiosity through the use of artifacts in teaching history. Through object-based teaching, students can begin to understand:

- how the past is different from the present,
- what changes have occurred over time,
- what has endured with little or no change over time and why,
- stereotyped views of the past, how they evolved, and the need for a more balanced view of the past,
- the relevance of major events and their causes and repercussions in relation to the individual and the world.

The following student activities will help to enhance students' understanding of the importance of history in their lives. They will also help students enjoy more fully their history museum field trip.

Learning to Look (Pre-visit or Museum Activity)

This can be done as an oral or a written activity in the classroom and followed up in the museum.

Begin by asking your students: What is an artifact? What is an authentic reproduction?

The word "artifact" comes from two Latin words—*ars,* which means art, and *facere,* which means to make. An artifact is something that has been produced by human work. An artifact is an original object from a particular period of history. An artifact has a story to tell, a history to reveal. By careful observation the story can be uncovered.

An "authentic reproduction" is an exact replica of an artifact. An authentic reproduction is often not created during the same period of history as the original artifact of which it is a copy.

Begin by selecting an object or document. Place the object or document where all the students can see it or gather round it. If you are going to do this activity orally, allow the students an opportunity to examine the selected object closely. Pass the object around so that all the students have an opportunity to hold it and examine it. Discuss with your students the definition of *artifact*. Then, ask the students the questions listed on the Student Investigation Worksheets for artifacts or for documents on pages 73–76.

If you choose to do this activity as a written exercise, copy the Student Investigation Worksheet for either artifacts or documents for each student. The worksheet can be used by students as a study tool to examine the selected object or document. The worksheet will provide students with guidelines to help them sharpen their observation skills.

A Three-Dimensional Time Line (Pre-visit Activity)

Collect several objects that reflect different time periods and technologies. If possible try to collect the same type of object—a selection of irons, for instance: an early cast iron used on a wood or coal stove, an early electric iron, a contemporary iron. Place the objects on a table and ask the students to create a time line using them. Then discuss each object with the students including how it reflects the time period in which it was created and the type of technology it represents. Compare each object to the one next to it on the time line. How are they similar? How are they different? What inventions or improvements in technology changed the object? How can you tell if one object is older than another?

This activity can be done with pictures if you cannot secure the actual three-dimensional objects. Here are some ideas for your time line:

- scrub brush and bucket, washboard, ringer washing machine, modern washing machine

- clothespin, drying rack for clothes, early dryer, modern dryer, dry cleaner

- quill pen and inkwell, fountain pen, ballpoint pen, disposable pen, felt-tip pen, fashion pen

From *The Field Trip Handbook* by Genean Stec, published by Good Year Books. Copyright © 1992 Chester County Intermediate Unit.

Cross Cultural Comparison (Pre-visit or Museum Activity)

Select an object (contemporary or antique) used by a particular cultural or ethnic group. Discuss with the students whether it has a counterpart in other cultures. Compare the object with its counterpart. How are they similar? How are they different? Are they still used by the different cultural groups today? Why or why not? If there is no counterpart, discuss the reasons why.

Here are suggestions for cross cultural comparisons:

- kitchen utensils
- kitchen equipment
- bedroom furniture, types and styles of beds
- transportation, vehicles
- architecture, home and office buildings

What Does this Object Say About Us? (Pre-visit Activity and Museum Activity)

Select a contemporary object. Discuss the following questions with the students.

1. What ideas, values, or customs does this object represent in our society?
2. What value do you personally attach to this object?
3. Why is this object important to you?
4. Will this object always be important to you?
5. Will this object's importance to you change as you get older? Will it become more valuable or less valuable to you? Why?

The next part of the activity can be done in the classroom or at the museum. Contact the museum's education department to see if it has objects from another culture or historic period to lend to schools for classroom use. If not, ask for suggestions of objects and information about them that would be appropriate for this activity.

Select a historic object. Discuss the following questions with the students.

1. What ideas, values, or customs does this object represent in the culture or historic period from which it came?
2. Was this object of great importance to the culture or historic period in which it was created and used? Why or why not?
3. To whom was this object of greatest importance? Explain your answer.
4. Is this object still used today? Why or why not?

Films and Videos (Pre-visit or Post-visit Activity)

Contact your film librarian to get a list of films or videos related to your field trip topic. Show a film or video to your students before their field trip. Upon your return, have them compare and contrast the film with their field trip experience.

Which provided more information on the particular historic topic selected? Which was more interesting to the students? Why? What does their choice reflect about their life-styles and values?

Cause and Effect (Pre-visit, Museum, and Post-visit Activity)

Pre-visit component
Create a list of historic events that are related to your field trip topic. Allow each student to select an event of interest from the list. Before the field trip, discuss with the students the significance of each event.

Museum component
During the visit, each student should gather five pieces of information related to the cause of the historic event he or she selected and a list of facts to support the cause. Each student should also gather a list of five effects of the historic event on the people and things of that period.

Post-visit component
Back in the classroom, have the students pretend they lived in the time periods of their chosen events. Each should write a letter to a friend or relative describing his or her historic event. In the letters they should mention some of the causes of the events and how their lives were affected.

Controversy (Pre-visit, Museum, and Post-visit Activity)

Pre-visit component: Collecting the Facts
Many historic events are surrounded by controversial issues. Select a historic event related to your field trip topic. Discuss with your students the historic event and the controversies surrounding it. Instruct the students to choose a side of the controversy to research. Students can be either pro or con. Allow the students an opportunity to gather information to support their stands. Remind them to consider the causes and effects of the event when researching their stands.

Museum component: Taking Sides
Allow the students an opportunity during their museum experience to gather additional information to support their arguments. Students should use the museum staff, exhibits, and artifacts to gather information. Each student should gather at least five facts during the museum visit.

Post-visit component: The Great Debate
Back in the classroom, provide the students with an opportunity to organize the information they collected into short speeches to support their stands. Divide the students into two groups, pro and con. Have each group take turns presenting

From *The Field Trip Handbook* by Genean Stec, published by Good Year Books. Copyright © 1992 Chester County Intermediate Unit.

speeches. When students have completed their presentations, sum up the debate and discuss with them the importance of considering all sides of the issue. Take a poll. Were any of the students persuaded to change their positions after the debate? If so, have them explain their reasons for changing their minds.

The Historian as Poet (Pre-visit, Museum, and Post-visit Activity)

Pre-visit component
Create a list of significant people, places, or events that students will learn about during their visit to the history museum. Ask each student to select a topic of interest from the list. Allow them an opportunity to gather five facts about the historic people, places, or events they selected using their textbooks or resources found in the school library.

Museum component
During their field trip, create an opportunity for the students to gather five more facts about the topics they selected. While looking at exhibits related to their topics, have the students list ten adjectives to describe their topics.

Post-visit component
Back in the classroom, have the students create lists of five people, places, events, or characteristics that are the opposite of or in contrast to those of their topics. Then have the students create simple poems, similes, or metaphors related to their topics using the information they gathered. Have them share their poetry with their classmates. Ask the students to create drawings to illustrate their poems. Design a bulletin board display using the poems and illustrations.

Have the students use the worksheet on page 77 to collect their information.

Researching the Past (Post-visit Activity)

In a class discussion after the field trip, make a list of the historic topics, persons, or events touched upon during the visit. Have each student select a historic topic, person, or event of interest from this list. Visit your school library and have the librarian introduce the students to the library and the various resources available for research purposes, such as the card file, clipping files, and reference books. Discuss with the students the difference between primary and secondary resources. Then instruct the students to research their topics using at least one primary source along with two secondary sources. Have each student present an oral report to the class on the information discovered and the types of resources used. The worksheet on page 79 can be used as a tool to help the students collect and record their research. If your students are older, instruct them on the proper way to record a bibliographic note using notecards.

Replicating the Past (Post-visit Activity)

Have students create drawings, dioramas, or models of events or inventions of historical significance covered during your field trip experience.

Digging for Clues to the Past (Pre-visit, Museum, and Post-visit Activity)

Pre-visit component
Divide the students into small research teams. Have each group of students write five questions it would like to ask a particular historic figure who will be discussed during the upcoming field trip.

Museum component
During the field trip, give the students an opportunity to collect information that might help them answer their questions from label copy in the exhibition, objects in the museum, or their museum interpreter.

Post-visit component
Back in the classroom, have the students share their questions and the answers they collected. Discuss with them how they might find the answers to any unanswered questions. (Use materials found in the archives or library such as letters, journals, or period newspapers; talk with the museum curator; read a biography or autobiography on the particular person; interview any surviving family members or friends.)

In My Opinion

Back in the classroom, make a list with your students of the five most important historical events or historical figures covered during the field trip. Instruct each student to select one event or person of interest from the list. Tell the students to pretend that they witnessed the event or knew the person. Have each student write a letter to a friend or relative describing the event or person. Select several students to share their letters with the class.

As a class, make a list of the points concerning each event or person that are mentioned repeatedly in the students' letters. Make a list of the unique points mentioned in only one or two of the students' letters.

Discuss with your students how eyewitness accounts of an event or person can be different and what effect this has on the interpretation of past events and persons.

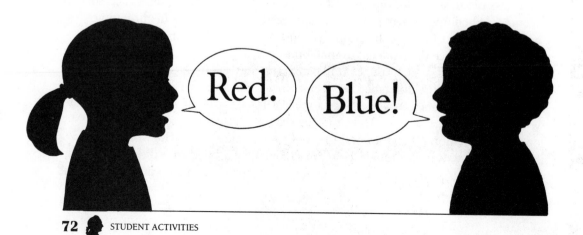

From *The Field Trip Handbook* by Genean Stec, published by Good Year Books. Copyright © 1992 Chester County Intermediate Unit.

Learning to Look

Student Investigation Worksheet for Documents

Primary Source: An object, document, or firsthand account from the time period under discussion

Secondary Source: A secondhand object, document, or account created by people who were not part of the past event. These sources are one step removed from an event because they are neither products of the event nor eyewitness reports. Secondary sources may vary widely in their interpretations of an event.

Types of Sources:
drawings
photographs
three-dimensional objects
printed materials
manuscripts—handwritten or typed material that has never been published
oral histories—personal recollections or statements from individuals, either tape-recorded, videotaped, or in written form

Name of the document: _____

As you examine this document, ask yourself these questions.

1. Who wrote or drew this document? _____

2. When and where was it written or drawn? _____

_____

3. How close was the writer or artist to the event described?

_____

4. Who was the intended audience?

_____

73

5. Was the writer or artist trying to promote a specific point of view? (opinion or bias)

_____

What was the point of view?

_____

_____

6. Briefly describe and/or sketch the document.

7. List three characteristics that you feel are important to know about the document. Please explain your answer.

_____

_____

8. On a scale of 1 to 10, where would you rank this document for truth and reliability? Please explain your choice.

1   2   3   4   5   6   7   8   9   10
Not Reliable   Very Reliable

_____

_____

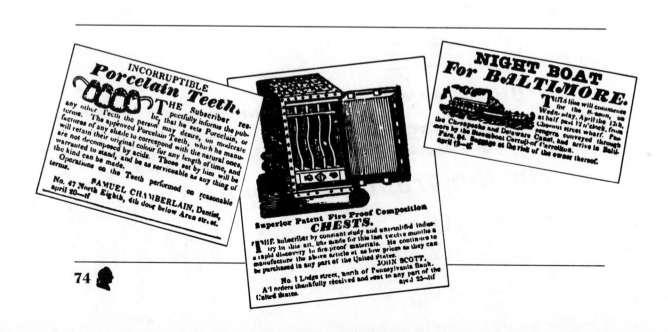

From *The Field Trip Handbook* by Genean Stec, published by Good Year Books. Copyright © 1992 Chester County Intermediate Unit.

Name _____   Date _____

Learning to Look

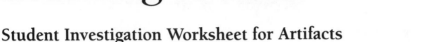

Student Investigation Worksheet for Artifacts

Primary Source: An object, document, or firsthand account from the time period under discussion.

Secondary Source: A secondhand object, document, or account created by people who were not part of the past event. These sources are one step removed from an event because they are neither products of the event nor eyewitness reports. Secondary sources may vary widely in their interpretations of an event.

Types of Sources:
drawings
photographs
three-dimensional objects
printed materials
manuscripts—handwritten or typed material that has never been published
oral histories—personal recollections or statements from individuals, either tape-recorded, videotaped, or in written form

Name of the artifact: _____

As you examine this artifact, ask yourself these questions.

1. What type of source is this artifact? _____

2. When was the artifact made? (approximately) _____

3. Who made the artifact? _____

4. How was the artifact made? _____

    Of what material(s) is the artifact made? _____

    Is the artifact handmade or machine made? Explain your answer. _____

    _____

5. How might this artifact have been used?

_____

What is the purpose of the artifact?

_____

Who used this artifact?

_____

6. Briefly describe the artifact.

_____

7. List three characteristics that you feel are important to know about the artifact. Please explain your answer.

_____

_____

_____

8. Sketch a picture of the artifact.

9. What can you determine about the life-style of the people who used this artifact?

_____

_____

From *The Field Trip Handbook* by Genean Stec, published by Good Year Books. Copyright © 1992 Chester County Intermediate Unit.

Name _____   Date _____

The Historian as Poet

Topic: _____

Five facts about the topic:

1. _____

2. _____

3. _____

4. _____

5. _____

At the museum collect five more facts about the topic.

1. _____

2. _____

3. _____

4. _____

5. _____

While looking closely and carefully at the exhibit and objects related to the topic, list ten adjectives that describe the topic.

1. _____	6. _____
2. _____	7. _____
3. _____	8. _____
4. _____	9. _____
5. _____	10. _____

From *The Field Trip Handbook* by Genean Stec, published by Good Year Books. Copyright © 1992 Chester County Intermediate Unit.

Back in the classroom, create a list of five people, places, events, adjectives, or characteristics that are opposite of or in contrast to the topic.

1. _____

2. _____

3. _____

4. _____

5. _____

Using all the information collected above, create a simple poem, a simile, or a metaphor related to the topic.

Create a drawing to illustrate your poem.

From *The Field Trip Handbook* by Genean Stec, published by Good Year Books. Copyright © 1992 Chester County Intermediate Unit.

Name _____ Date _____

Researching the Past

Research topic: _____

Primary sources used: _____

_____

_____

Information collected from these sources:

_____

_____

_____

Secondary sources used:

1. _____

Information collected from this source:

_____

_____

_____

2. _____

Information collected from this source:

_____

_____

_____

SCIENCE MUSEUMS

Activities and Worksheets

"Science museum" is a term used here to describe a rich variety of educational institutions whose focus is science. These museums can provide a teacher with a wealth of information and educational opportunities to enhance the teaching of such subjects as natural science, earth science, astronomy, and physical science.

The following student activities have been designed to work in a variety of science museums. Several of the student activities found in the sections on art and history can also be adapted for use on field trips to science museums. These include:

Art
Getting to Know an Artist
Clues
Favorites

History
Learning to Look
Historian as Poet
Researching the Past
Digging for Clues to the Past

How Carefully Do You Observe? (Pre-visit or Museum Activity)

This activity is best done in the museum but it can be done in the classroom before the field trip. It is intended to help sharpen students' observation skills and to introduce them to the field trip's topic. Make a copy of the worksheet on page 85 for each student. Students may work separately or in small groups to complete this activity.

Select several objects for the students to examine that relate to the field trip topic. If you cannot visit the museum to select the objects in advance, ask a museum educator to suggest some appropriate objects. If you choose to do the activity in the classroom, inquire as to whether the museum would loan you several objects. Many museums have educational collections that they are willing to loan to teachers for classroom use.

From *The Field Trip Handbook* by Genean Stec, published by Good Year Books. Copyright © 1992 Chester County Intermediate Unit.

Questions, Questions, and More Questions (Museum and Post-visit Activity)

Museum component
Visit the science museum and meet with the museum educator to review your field trip plans. Request information form the education department on exhibits and activities related to your field trip topic. Using this information and after examining the exhibits yourself, create a question for each student to answer during the field trip. Create a mixture of both objective and subjective questions. Write each question on a large index card. During the trip, each student will be responsible for finding the answer to his or her question.

Post-visit component
After the field trip, use the questions and answers to review your experience. Have the students share their findings with one another.

Using Your Senses to Discover the World: Touch It! (Pre-visit Activity)

Select several objects related to the scientific topic of the upcoming field trip. Choose objects that are interesting to touch. Put each object in a large paper bag or box. Have the students take turns reaching into the bags or boxes to feel the objects without looking at them. After the students have had an opportunity to examine the objects using only their sense of touch, have them complete the student worksheet on page 87 for each object.

From *The Field Trip Handbook* by Genean Stec; published by Good Year Books. Copyright © 1992 Chester County Intermediate Unit.

Using Your Senses to Discover the World: Smell It! (Pre-visit Activity)

Select several objects related to the scientific topic of your upcoming field trip. Choose objects that are interesting to smell. Put each object in a small box or film canister with holes punched in the lid. Have the students take turns smelling boxes; they should not be able to see or touch the objects. After the students have had an opportunity to examine the objects using only their sense of smell, have them complete the worksheet on page 88 for each object. If possible, challenge the class with about ten different fragrances. Keep pictures of each object in reserve. After the students complete the worksheets, see if they can match each fragrance with the appropriate picture. (Some suggestions for fragrances are spices or herbs such as cinnamon, cloves, or basil; fresh orange, lemon, or tangerine peels; fresh pine needles; fresh flowers; and freshly ground coffee.)

Creating an Exhibition (Pre-visit or Post-visit Activity)

This activity can be done either as an introduction to your field trip topic or as a review and wrap-up of your field trip experience. It can take the form of a group discussion or an individual written exercise. For either format, use the worksheet on page 89 as a guideline.

Select an object related to your field trip topic. If you cannot get the actual object, use a picture, slide, or poster of the object. Place it where all the students can see it. Discuss with the students the significance of this object.

How is it used?

How was it made?

How does it relate to the field trip topic?

How does it relate to the science lesson?

From *The Field Trip Handbook* by Genean Stec, published by Good Year Books. Copyright © 1992 Chester County Intermediate Unit.

How Am I Different? (Pre-visit, Museum, and Post-visit Activity for a natural history museum)

Pre-visit component
Have each student select an animal that he or she is interested in researching. Using textbooks and the school library, have students list ten facts about their animals on the worksheet on page 91.

Museum component
During their visit to the museum, have students carefully observe the animals they selected and list five significant characteristics. Have the students gather information about their animals' senses. What does each animal use to taste, touch, smell, see, and hear?

Post-visit component
Back in the classroom, have the students compare the animals' senses to their own in a written exercise. How does the student taste, touch, smell, see, and hear? How are the student's senses similar to the animal's senses? How are the student's senses different from the animal's senses? What advantages do the animal's senses have over the student's senses? What advantages do the student's senses have over the animal's senses?

For each component, use the worksheet on page 91.

Inventions! (Pre-visit, Museum, and Post-visit Activity)

Pre-visit component
Create a list of inventions that the students will see during their field trip to the science museum. Ask each student to select an invention from the list that he or she is interested in learning more about. Using their textbooks and the school library, have students create lists of five facts related to their inventions.

Museum component
During the museum experience, allow the students an opportunity to gather more information about their inventions. Ask the students to list five facts related to the history of the inventions and five facts related to the effect the inventions had on people's lives.

Post-visit component
Back in the classroom, have the students pretend they are newspaper reporters. Have them write short articles on their "new" inventions using the information they collected. As a review of the field-trip experience, have the students share their articles with one another.

Use the worksheet on page 93 as a guideline for this activity.

From *The Field Trip Handbook* by Genean Stec, published by Good Year Books. Copyright © 1992 Chester County Intermediate Unit.

The Mad Scientists (Post-visit Activity)

After your museum visit, have your students create a list of scientific problems discussed during the museum experience. Using the worksheet on page 94, have them select a problem from this list and create an invention to solve it. Then have the students share their inventions with one another and create an exhibition of all these new inventions. Invite other classes to tour the exhibition.

From *The Field Trip Handbook* by Genean Stec, published by Good Year Books. Copyright © 1992 Chester County Intermediate Unit.

Name _____ Date _____

How Carefully Do You Observe?

For one minute, carefully observe _____
Now turn away and answer the following questions.

1. Describe the object.

_____

_____

2. Draw a sketch of the object.

3. What are three significant features of the object?

_____

_____

_____

4. List the various materials from which the object is made.

_____

_____

From *The Field Trip Handbook* by Genean Stec, published by Good Year Books. Copyright © 1992 Chester County Intermediate Unit.

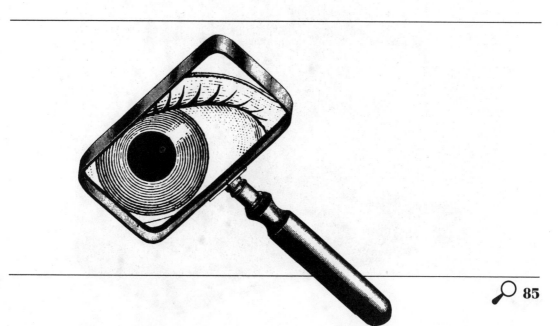

5. What color(s) is the object? _____

6. Does the object have moving parts? If so, name these parts.

    _____

    _____

7. Is the object powered by an energy source? If so, what type of energy?

    _____

8. What is the purpose of this object?

    _____

9. When was this object made? _____

10. When you have completed the questions, face the object and check your answers. How
    many questions did you answer correctly and completely? Rate your observation skills
    on the scale below.

1	2	3	4	5
poor		average		good

From *The Field Trip Handbook* by Genean Stec, published by Good Year Books. Copyright © 1992 Chester County Intermediate Unit.

Name _____ Date _____

Using Your Senses to Discover the World: Touch It!

Examine the object in the bag or box using only your sense of touch. Do not look at the object.

1. After you have examined the object, draw a picture of it.

2. List the different textures you felt on the object.

_____

_____

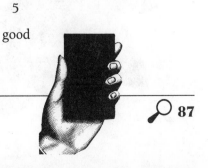

3. From what materials do you think the object is made?

_____

_____

4. Is the object natural, human-made, or machine-made? _____

5. What do you think this object is?

_____

6. How many uses can you think of for this object?

_____

_____

7. After completing the above questions, discuss your answers with your classmates. After everyone has had a chance to share their observations open the bag or box and look at the object. How carefully did you observe with your hands? Rate yourself on the scale below.

1	2	3	4	5
poor		average		good

From *The Field Trip Handbook* by Genean Stec, published by Good Year Books. Copyright © 1992 Chester County Intermediate Unit.

Using Your Senses to Discover the World: Smell It!

1. After smelling the fragrance in the box, what do you think the object is?

    _____

2. Is it a natural or human-made fragrance? _____

3. How is it used? Does it have a purpose?

    _____

    _____

4. Where is it found in this world?

    _____

5. What would happen if this fragrance disappeared? How would it affect the object(s) to which it is related?

    _____

    _____

    _____

From *The Field Trip Handbook* by Genean Stec, published by Good Year Books. Copyright © 1992 Chester County Intermediate Unit.

From *The Field Trip Handbook* by Genean Stec, published by Good Year Books. Copyright © 1992 Chester County Intermediate Unit.

Name _____   Date _____

Creating an Exhibition

Pretend that you are a curator in a science museum and that you have been instructed by the director of the museum to create an exhibition in which this object is featured prominently. Answer the following questions.

What kinds of exhibitions might include such an object? List three possible themes.

1. _____

2. _____

3. _____

Select one of the themes from your list and answer the following questions.

Theme: _____

What are the three most important pieces of information to convey when you exhibit this object?

1. _____

2. _____

3. _____

Describe how you would exhibit the object.

_____

_____

_____

_____

Name five objects you would like to include in your exhibition to help depict the importance of this object.

1. _____

2. _____

3. _____

4. _____

5. _____

What special program or activity would you design for students related to your exhibition and the object?

_____

_____

What would you name your exhibition?

_____

From *The Field Trip Handbook* by Genean Stec, published by Good Year Books. Copyright © 1992 Chester County Intermediate Unit.

Name _____   Date _____

How Am I Different?

Select an animal that you are interested in learning more about from the list provided by your teacher.

Animal: _____

Using your textbook and the school library, list ten facts about this animal.

1. _____

2. _____

3. _____

4. _____

5. _____

6. _____

7. _____

8. _____

9. _____

10. _____

During your museum or zoo visit, carefully investigate exhibits dealing with your animal and read the related labels. Then list five significant characteristics regarding the animal's senses. Look carefully at the animal's nose, ears, and eyes.

1. _____

2. _____

3. _____

4. _____

5. _____

🔍 91

From *The Field Trip Handbook* by Genean Stec, published by Good Year Books. Copyright © 1992 Chester County Intermediate Unit.

Look carefully at your animal and answer the following questions.

How does the animal smell? _____

How does the animal taste? _____

How does the animal hear? _____

How does the animal see? _____

How does the animal touch? _____

Does the animal have any special sensory adaptations? _____

_____

Back in the classroom, compare the animal's use of its senses to yourself.

List three ways that you and the animal are similar in your use of the senses.

1. _____

2. _____

3. _____

List three ways that you and the animal are different in your use of the senses.

1. _____

2. _____

3. _____

Write a short story describing a school day during which you had the animal's senses instead of your own.

_____

_____

_____

_____

_____

_____

_____

From *The Field Trip Handbook* by Genean Stec, published by Good Year Books. Copyright © 1992 Chester County Intermediate Unit.

From *The Field Trip Handbook* by Genean Stec, published by Good Year Books. Copyright © 1992 Chester County Intermediate Unit.

Name _____   Date _____

Inventions!

Select an invention from the teacher's list that you are interested in learning more about.

Invention: _____

Using your textbook and the school library, create a list of five facts related to this invention.

1. _____

2. _____

3. _____

4. _____

5. _____

During your museum visit, gather more information about your invention by carefully examining the object and reading the label copy related to it.

List five new facts about the history of the invention.

1. _____

2. _____

3. _____

4. _____

5. _____

List three facts related to the effect the invention had on people's lives.

1. _____

2. _____

3. _____

Draw a picture of your invention on a separate sheet of paper.

Back in the classroom, pretend that you are a newspaper reporter and that this invention has just been presented to the world. Write a short article on this new invention using the information you collected. How has this invention changed the world? Why is it so important?

_____

Name _____   Date _____

The Mad Scientists

Select a scientific problem that interests you from the list drawn from your museum experience by you and your classmates.

The scientific problem is: _____

_____

_____

Create an invention to solve this scientific problem. Briefly describe your invention and how it works.

_____

_____

_____

_____

Draw a picture of your invention or create a model.

As a class create an exhibit of all these new inventions. Invite students in your school to come and tour your exhibit.

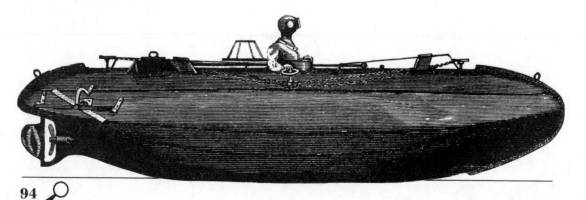

Chapter 5
Evaluate the Field Trip

Evaluation is an important component of all learning experiences. Through evaluation one can learn the strengths and weaknesses of a program and make the necessary changes in later programs. Every effort should be made to evaluate all field trip experiences. The thoughtful review of a field trip by teachers, chaperons, and students can provide many helpful suggestions. Take the time to share these suggestions with the museum's education department.

Included here are evaluation forms for all participating teachers, chaperons, and students. As the planner, be sure to evaluate the trip yourself on the teachers' form.

From *The Field Trip Handbook* by Genean Stec, published by Good Year Books. Copyright © 1992 Chester County Intermediate Unit.

Teachers' Field Trip Evaluation Form

Your help in making our class field trip a success is greatly appreciated. To meet the educational goals and objectives of this field trip, your valuable feedback is needed. Please take the time to complete this evaluation and return it to:

_____

1. Did you study the topic with your students prior to the museum experience?

2. Did you use any of the pre-visit student activities with your class prior to the museum experience? Why or why not?

    If you did use a pre-visit activity, which did you use? Was it helpful in preparing your students? Why or why not?

3. Did you use any of the museum activities? Why or why not?

    If you did use a museum activity, which activity did you use? Was it helpful in rounding out the students' museum experience?

4. Did you use any of the post-visit activities? Why or why not?

    If you did use a post-visit activity, which activity did you use? Was it helpful in providing a wrap-up of your museum experience?

5. Did the museum provide you with enough information to prepare you and your students for their museum experience?

6. Please circle the word that best describes your students' museum experience.

   disaster   unsuccessful   average   good   excellent

   Please explain your answer.

7. What improvements would you suggest to make the museum experience better? Please be as specific as you can in your suggestions.

8. Would you schedule this program again? Why or why not?

9. Would you recommend this program to other teachers? Why or why not?

10. What changes would you recommend to improve the entire field trip experience (including the transportation to and from the museum, lunch, and the museum experience)?

11. How could you have better prepared for the field trip experience?

12. Did you meet the educational goals and objectives set for the field trip? Why or why not?

13. Do you have any additional comments and suggestions?

From *The Field Trip Handbook* by Genean Stec, published by Good Year Books. Copyright © 1992 Chester County Intermediate Unit.

Chaperons' Field Trip Evaluation Form

Your help in making our class field trip a success is greatly appreciated. To meet the educational goals and objectives of this field trip, your valuable feedback is needed. Please take the time to complete this evaluation and return it to:

_____

_____

_____

Chaperon: (optional)_____

1. Did the teacher provide you with enough information prior to the field trip concerning the day's schedule and your responsibilities?

2. Please circle the word that best describes your museum experience with the students.

   disaster   unsuccessful   average   good   excellent

   Please explain your answer.

3. What improvements or changes would you suggest to make the museum experience better? Please be as specific as you can in your suggestions.

4. What museum experience do you feel the students enjoyed the most? Please explain your answer.

5. What museum experience do you feel the students enjoyed the least? Please explain your answer.

6. Did you feel the museum interpreter presented the material at the students' level? Did he or she have a good rapport with the students? Please explain your answer.

7. Would you participate as a chaperon again? Why or why not?

8. Would you recommend this museum experience to other teachers? Why or why not?

9. What changes would you recommend to improve the entire field trip experience (including the transportation to and from the museum, lunch, and the museum experience)?

10. Would you have liked to attend a chaperons' meeting to prepare you for the field trip experiences?

11. Do you have any additional comments and suggestions?

From *The Field Trip Handbook* by Genean Stec, published by Good Year Books. Copyright © 1992 Chester County Intermediate Unit.

From *The Field Trip Handbook* by Genean Stec, published by Good Year Books. Copyright © 1992 Chester County Intermediate Unit.

Name _____   Date _____

Student's Field Trip Evaluation Form

Field Trip Date: _____   Museum Visited: _____

1. Did you enjoy your museum experience? Why or why not?

_____

_____

2. Which activity was your favorite? Why?

_____

_____

3. Which activity was your least favorite? Why?

_____

_____

4. If you could change something about your museum experience, what would you change? Why?

_____

_____

5. Did you do any activities in your classroom before you went to the museum that helped prepare you for your museum experience?

_____

If yes, what kind of activities did you do?

_____

_____

6. Did you do any activities in your classroom after you returned from the field trip?

    _____

    If yes, what activities did you do?

    _____

7. Would you go back to the museum with your family and friends? Why or why not?

    _____

8. Describe one thing you learned during your museum experience.

    _____

    _____

From *The Field Trip Handbook* by Genean Stec, published by Good Year Books. Copyright © 1992 Chester County Intermediate Unit.

Chapter 6
Where to Go for More Help

Bibliography

Abhau, Marcy, Rolaine Copeland, and Greta Greenberger, eds. *Architecture in Education: A Resource of Imaginative Ideas and Tested Activities.* Philadelphia, PA: The Foundation for Architecture Philadelphia, 1986.

Alexander, Edward P. *Museums in Motion: An Introduction to the History and Functions of Museums.* Nashville, TN: American Association for State and Local History, 1979.

Booth, Jeanette Hauck, et al. *Creative Museum Methods and Educational Techniques.* Springfield, IL: Charles C. Thomas, 1982.

Feldman, Edmund Burke. *Becoming Human Through Art, Aesthetic Experience in the School.* Englewood Cliffs, NJ: Prentice-Hall, 1970.

Grinder, Alison L., and E. Sue McCoy. *The Good Guide: A Sourcebook for Interpreters, Docents and Tour Guides.* Scottsdale, AZ: Ironwood Publishing, 1985.

Nichols, Susan K., ed., Mary Alexander and Ken Yellis, assoc. eds. *Museum Education Anthology 1973–1983, Perspectives on Informal Learning a Decade of Roundtable Reports.* Washington, DC: Museum Education Roundtable, 1984.

Pitman-Gelles, Bonnie. *Museums, Magic and Children.* Washington, DC: Association of Science-Technology Centers, 1981.

Schlereth, Thomas J. *Artifacts and the American Past.* Nashville, TN: American Association for State and Local History, 1980.

Taylor, Joshua C. *Learning to Look: A Handbook for the Visual Arts.* Chicago, IL: The University of Chicago Press, 1957.

Voris, Helen H. *Teach the Mind Touch the Spirit: A Guide to Focused Field Trips.* Chicago, IL: Department of Education, Field Museum of Natural History, 1986.

Resources

The American Institute of Architects
Senior Director of Education Programs
1735 New York Avenue NW
Washington, DC 20006
202–626–7300

AIA's environmental education program, Learning by Design, is a system of resources designed to enable educators to develop an enhanced perception of their surroundings and translate those perceptions into practical activities for their students. The AIA's *The Sourcebook II* is a comprehensive and convenient reference book for teaching at all learning levels, from kindergarten through adult education. For more information about *The Sourcebook II* or your regional coordinator, please contact Alan R. Sandler at AIA.

Anthro Notes
Public Information Office
Department of Anthropology
National Museum of Natural History
Smithsonian Institution
Washington, DC 20560

Anthro Notes is a newsletter for teachers produced by the National Museum of Natural History. It is available free of charge three times a year.

Archeological Assistance Division
National Park Service
P.O. Box 3727
Washington, DC 20013-7127
202–343–4101

The Archeological Assistance Division has prepared a resource packet for teachers. Its purpose is to identify for teachers some of the educational material about archeology and archeological methods and techniques that are available for classroom use. The division has also created a database of summary information about public education efforts in archeological projects. This database, the Listing of Education in Archeological Projects (LEAP), is available by writing to the division.

Beyond the Blackboard: A Guide to Regional Museum Resources
Louise Hartman
The Woodmere Art Museum
9201 Germantown Avenue
Philadelphia, PA 19118
215–247–0476

This regional guide reviews over seventy-five museums and cultural institutions in the Philadelphia and Delaware Valley area, providing information on school programs and available facilities. The cost of the book is $7 per single copy; bulk-rate discounts are available.

From *The Field Trip Handbook* by Genean Stec, published by Good Year Books. Copyright © 1992 Chester County Intermediate Unit.

Coordinator of Teacher Workshops and Materials
Department of Teacher and School Programs
National Gallery of Art
Washington, DC 20565
202–842–6875

Resources available for teachers free of charge from the National Gallery include color slide programs, films, and video cassettes. For a free catalog describing the offerings and procedures for ordering materials call 202–842–6273 or write Extension Programs Section, Department of Education, National Gallery of Art, Washington, DC 20565.

CUBE, Center for Understanding the Built Environment
5328 W. Sixty-seventh Street
Prairie Village, KS 66208
913–262–0691

ArchiNet, a part of CUBE, is an organization of teachers, architects, and citizens networking for built environment awareness education. Members of ArchiNet receive a host of educational benefits which include: *ArchiNews,* a newsletter that links all of those working in heritage education and the built environment; special notices of courses and workshops; training in the Polaroid Education Foundation program; ArchiSource catalogs filled with the latest architectural resources; and the privilege of checking out videos, slides, and architectural toys. For more information, contact the membership coordinator at ArchiNet by writing or calling CUBE.

Elementary Science Outreach Program
Museum of Science Park
Boston, MA 02114–1099
1–800–722–KITS

The Elementary Science Outreach Program provides science kits filled with ideas, materials, and activities for a class of up to thirty students plus a teacher's guide with instructions and supplies for each student. Topics include insects, birds, dinosaurs, plants and seeds, electricity, solar systems, simple machines, ancient Egypt, rocks and minerals, and wolves and humans.

Franklin Activity Kits
Science Kit and Borcal Laboratories
777 East Park Drive
Tonawanda, NY 14150
1–800–828–7777

The Franklin Institute's activity kits include all of the science materials and instructions needed to conduct a series of activities in each unit. Kits are designed to foster hands-on learning in a group setting. Kits cover life science, physical science, and earth science and include such topics as astronomy, meteorology, sound, energy, heat, light and color, ecosystems, and communities.

Harris Extension Program
Field Museum of Natural History
Roosevelt Road at Lake Shore Drive
Chicago, IL 60605
312–922–9410, extension 361

Loan materials available from the Harris Extension Program include audiovisual resources and exhibit cases and experience boxes on biology, botany, earth science, zoology, and social studies topics.

Metropolitan Museum of Art
Student and Teacher Programs
1000 Fifth Avenue
New York, NY 10028
212–570–3932

Teacher resource packets are available on several artistic styles and periods of art. A School Programs brochure is also available. It describes all the guided and self-guided student programs along with information on teacher workshops and in-service courses. For more information, call or write the museum at the above address.

Museum To Go Resource Center
The Franklin Institute Science Museum
Benjamin Franklin Parkway at Twentieth Street
Philadelphia, PA 19103-1194
215–448–1094

Through a variety of in-service workshops and instructional seminars sponsored by the Museum To Go Resource Center, teachers can enjoy opportunities to share scientific concepts and teaching methods while becoming more comfortable and confident teaching hands-on science.

National Teacher Institute
National Gallery of Art
Washington, DC 20565
202–842–6249

The National Gallery of Art has established an annual National Teacher Institute to prepare elementary- and secondary-level teachers to teach art and the humanities. The Institute, held in the summer, brings together teachers from across the country to learn, reflect, and share as professionals. It aims to refresh teachers and help them to maintain the excitement, inspiration, and creativity that excellent teaching requires.

Heritage Education Quarterly (HEQ)
The Preservation Library and Resource Center
498 South Main Street
Madison, GA 30650
404–342–0770

HEQ is a national newsletter that provides teachers and students with information on historic preservation and heritage education issues.

From *The Field Trip Handbook* by Genean Stec, published by Good Year Books. Copyright © 1992 Chester County Intermediate Unit.

From *The Field Trip Handbook* by Genean Stec, published by Good Year Books. Copyright © 1992 Chester County Intermediate Unit.

Science-By-Mail Program
Museum of Science Park
Boston, MA 02114–1099
1–800–729–3300

Anyone in grades four through nine can be a Scientist-By-Mail. The program enables students to correspond with scientists. Students can choose to work alone or in groups of four. Three science challenge packets are sent to the students. The packets are designed to allow students to work without supervision and at their own pace. The students have their own pen pal scientist and receive letters from them about their solutions to the challenges. Science-By-Mail programs follow the school calendar.

SITES
Publication Department
1100 Jefferson Drive SW
Room 3146
Washington, DC 20560
202–357–3168

The Smithsonian Institution Traveling Exhibition Service has a new publication for teachers which lists the rich variety of resources available for classroom use. *SITES Publication for Teachers* is a thirteen-page brochure and is available free of charge. The brochure lists by curriculum area numerous catalogs, posters, educational packets, and teacher guides available for purchase at a nominal charge. For more information call or write the above address.

Social Issues Resources Series, Inc.
P.O. Box 2348
Boca Raton, FL 33427
407–994–0079
1–800–232–SIRS

"SIRS Documents"—a collection of primary source documents—comprise supplemental teaching units prepared by educators at the National Archives. Each unit contains about fifty reproductions of documents—charts, photographs, letters, drawings, and posters. The materials deal with certain key issues in history and include governmental and political responses to the issues along with documents reflecting public attitudes. Topics include the Constitution, the Bill of Rights, the Civil War, the 1920s, World Wars I and II, and many more.

The Teacher's Resource Guide to the Smithsonian
Smithsonian Institution
Office of Elementary and Secondary Education (OESE)
Arts and Industries Building
Room 1163
Washington, DC 20560
202–357–2404

Traveling Science Shows
The Franklin Institute Science Museum
Benjamin Franklin Parkway at Twentieth Street
Philadelphia, PA 19103–1194
215–448–1110

The Franklin Institute's Traveling Science Shows are available to schools, youth groups, summer camps, recreation centers, and playgrounds from Virginia to New York, New Jersey to Ohio.

The Webber Resource Center
Native Cultures of the Americas
Field Museum of Natural History
Roosevelt Road at Lake Shore Drive
Chicago, IL 60605
312–922–9410, extension 497

The Webber Resource Center is a non-lending center which has a wealth of resources on the native cultures of North, South, and Central America. The materials available for use include activity boxes; videos; audiovisuals; books on the history, culture, and archaeology of native cultures; periodicals; newspapers; maps; photo albums; and basic reference books. If you're unable to visit, the Center's staff is most helpful collecting the requested information. For a brochure describing in detail the Webber Resource Center, call or write to the above address.

From *The Field Trip Handbook* by Genean Stec, published by Good Year Books. Copyright © 1992 Chester County Intermediate Unit.

Acknowledgments

Many of the illustrations in this book are from the following Dover publications:

1800 Woodcuts by Thomas Bewick and His School. New York: Dover Publications, Inc., 1962.

Animals: 1419 Copyright-Free Illustrations of Mammals, Birds, Fish, Insects, Etc. New York: Dover Publications, Inc., 1979.

Food and Drink: A Pictoral Archive from Nineteenth-Century Sources. New York: Dover Publications, Inc., 1983.

Goods and Merchandise: A Cornucopia of Nineteenth Century Cuts. New York: Dover Publications, Inc., 1982.

Handbook of Early Advertising Art. New York: Dover Publications, Inc., 1956.

Harter's Picture Archive for Collage and Illustration. New York: Dover Publications, Inc., 1978.

From *The Field Trip Handbook* by Genean Stec, published by Good Year Books. Copyright © 1992 Chester County Intermediate Unit.